How to Create & Understand Facebook Ads Simplified: A Step-by-Step Guide

- Easy step-by-step instructions for creating Facebook ads
- Learn how to understand Facebook ad reports
- Harness the power of Facebook audiences
- And Much More

Gary Starr

How to Create & Understand Facebook Ads Simplified
A Step-by-Step Guide

Published by Gary Starr

Copyright © 2018 Gary Starr
All rights reserved.

No part of this publication may be reproduced, stored in a retrieval system, or transmitted in any form or by any means --- electronic, mechanical, photocopy, recording, or any other – without the prior permission of the author.

Amazon ISBN: 9781729494899

Contents

Module 1 Introduction & Facebook Ad Manager……….1

Module 2 Creating a Basic Facebook Ad……………….. 17

Module 3 Facebook Ad Reports……………………...51

Module 4 Facebook Pixel & Basic Retargeting…………..64

Module 5 Custom Audiences……………………………72

Module 6 A/B Testing & Defining Audiences…………..86

Module 7 Facebook Ad Formats……………………...94

Module 8 Facebook Marketing Objectives……………….106

Module 9 Facebook Sales Funnel………………………..112

Module 10 Instagram Advertising………………………..117

About the Author…………………………………………..124

Module 1 Introduction & Facebook Ad Manager

Facebook is the behemoth of Social Media with 2.23 Billion active users who spend hours every day getting their daily fix of voyeurism into other people's lives. With that many eyeballs viewing their Facebook feeds, it has become the new informercial. Using the same formula as a late night informercial, those advertisers that are successful with Facebook ads identify the pain people are having and then find a solution to solve that pain causing an impulse buy. Everyone's #1 commodity is their time and Facebook users are more than willing to give it to you. So why aren't you advertising on Facebook and if you are why aren't you making money from your ads. Facebook is currently the cheapest way to advertise and the most effective way to reach your customer. There is absolutely no excuse not to be utilizing Facebook advertising to increase your sales and take your business to the next level. Just like informercials there is a serious amount of money to be made on Facebook.

The first step in making sure your journey is successful with Facebook advertising is to ensure you are not like everyone that is giving up their #1 commodity of time to unproductive endeavors such as spending time on Facebook or Social Media as an item of pleasure, Delete the Facebook app from your phone, turn off notifications from Facebook, don't use Facebook at work for personal items but only as a business tool and eliminate the temptation by closing the Facebook tab on your browser. Don't let Facebook distract you from your primary goal of producing excellent Facebook ads that will inevitably make you money.

So why should you be advertising on Facebook?

1. That is where your customers are! There is an argument constantly being tossed around that Facebook is dying or becoming obsolete but the opposite is the truth. Take a look at the below chart and you will see a healthy continued growth of Facebook. Any other business would love to have this type of growth.

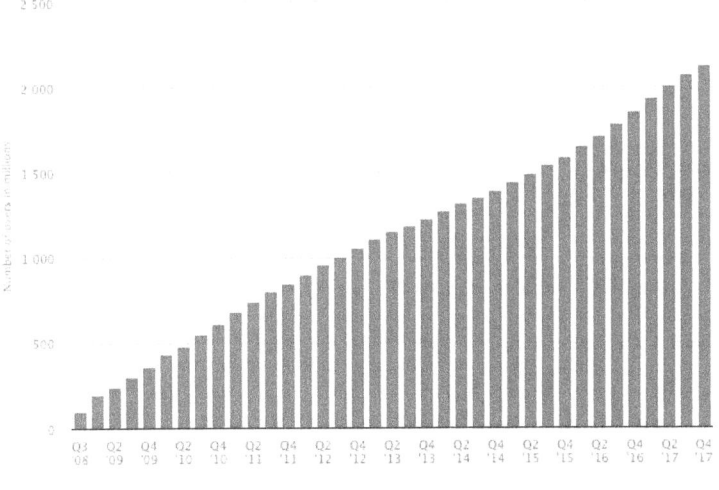

2. Facebook is a one stop shop for everything in a person's life. Besides offering the needed fix of voyeurism. Facebook also offers: check-ins at business and events, communication through messenger, sharing of photos, live video, registering for events and buying tickets for those events when connected with Eventbrite events, shopping and more. No other platform offers so much and Facebook is always adding more by acquiring other companies such as Instagram and WhatsApp.

3. Facebook rules the mobile device. Statistics show that people for the first time are using mobile devices more than desktop computers and laptops than ever before. The number would probably be even higher if people didn't have to use a desktop computer or laptop for work. Mobile device usage will continue to grow because who wants to lug a laptop to the pool or beach when you can carry a lightweight tablet or just your phone. Statistics show that 85% of Facebook advertising is occurring on the mobile device which people have with them 24/7.
4. Facebook advertising is inexpensive. You can start with as little as $10 a day advertising on Facebook and depending on your niche, your Cost per Click could be as low as .10 and shouldn't be over $1.00. Where else can you advertise and get potentially get around 100 new customers or leads a day for $10.
5. Facebook advertising is relatively easy to setup and get running. It doesn't require hiring a tech person to spend hours getting everything up and running in order to place your first Facebook ad. In addition, it is highly customizable, easy to do split testing, easy to reach your perfect audience with targeting and you are able to have trackable results. Tradition media is very tough to track if your ad dollars are being effective but with Facebook you can track exactly how much it costs to acquire a customer and pinpoint the best converting ads.
6. Facebook is the #1 way to build your email database and increase your leads for future customers. By creating the correct ad, you will be able to create a Sales Funnel with

inexpensive ads that will fill your funnel with warm leads. The goal is to find that one ad that will feed your funnel continually for months or years without having to touch it. This is known as an Evergreen because it goes on and on just like the Energizer Bunny.

Just with anything new you learn, you need to crawl first and then walk before you can expect to run. Don't get caught up in the instant gratification mentality that most people have these days. Your success is based on have a good understanding of the foundation of Facebook advertising and the proven techniques that others have pioneered. If you run out and just start running ads before knowing the foundation and just wing it, you will be wasting money and eventually be one of those who say Facebook ads don't work.

Each Facebook ad is also unique and what works for one person or business won't necessarily work for you. I've witnessed ads that I've run in various cities respond differently even though they are the same ad. I'm not saying using examples or templates is bad because sometimes you see something that causes a lightbulb to go off that you didn't see before and you can build off of these and make them better. Utilizing only examples or templates to build and run your ads will again cause you to waste a lot of money.

Not every ad will be a homerun but all it takes is one good ad to change your world. Don't get frustrated, learn the foundation of Facebook ads, continue to stay up to date with any changes and you will get the Evergreen ad that runs for months or even years without you having to touch it that much and that will bring in a constant flow of money.

Now that you see why you should be advertising on Facebook, how do you get started? The first thing you need to do is create a Business Facebook page. I'm going to assume you don't have one yet and will start there but if you already have a Business Facebook page you can skip to setting up your Facebook Ad Manager. This will won't take very long and will be a painless process. To prepare for creating your Business Facebook page and ensure things don't take too long, you may want to ensure you have your Business Profile Picture(180x180 pixels) and Facebook Cover Photo(828x315 pixels) ready before you start.

1. Create your Business Facebook page.
    a. Open up your personal Facebook page, click on the gear(Settings and Account) in top right of your page and then click on Create Page.

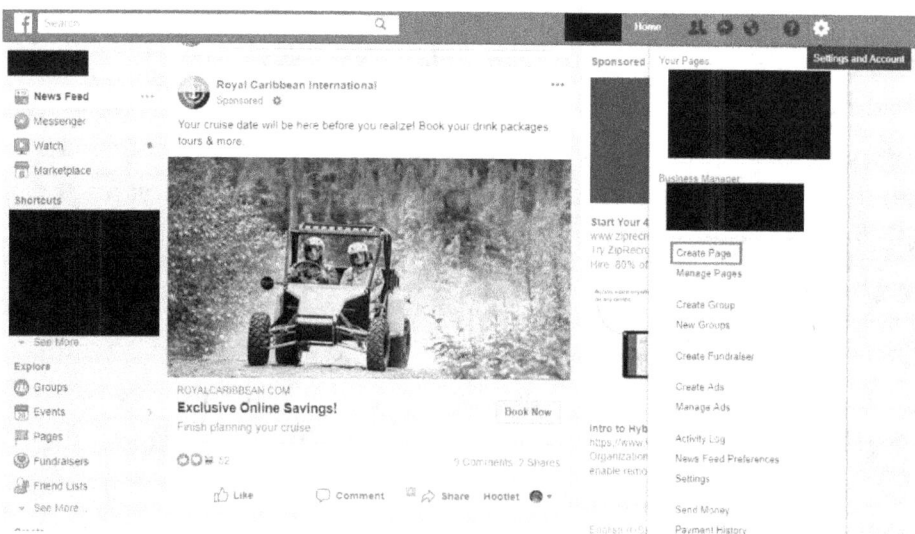

b. Click on Get Started under Business or Brand

Create a Page

Connect your business, yourself or your cause to the worldwide community of people on Facebook. To get started, choose a Page category.

Business or Brand

Showcase your products and services, spotlight your brand and reach more customers on Facebook.

Get Started

Community or Public Figure

Connect and share with people in your community, organization, team, group or club.

Get Started

c. Give your page a name and start typing the category your business would fit and Facebook will give you options. Then click Continue

Create a Page

Connect your business, yourself or your cause to the worldwide community of people on Facebook. To get started, choose a Page category.

Business or Brand

Connect with customers, grow your audience and showcase your products with a free business Page.

Page Name
Your Company Name
Category
Product/Service

When you create a Page on Facebook the Pages, Groups and Events Policies apply.

Continue

Community or Public Figure

Connect and share with people in your community, organization, team, group or club

Get Started

d. Upload your profile picture. Facebook profile pictures should be 180x180 pixels in size.

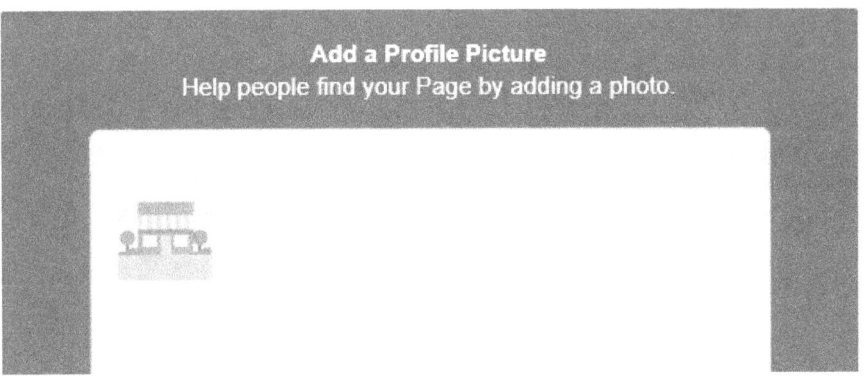

e. Upload your cover photo. Facebook cover photos should be 828x315 pixels in size.

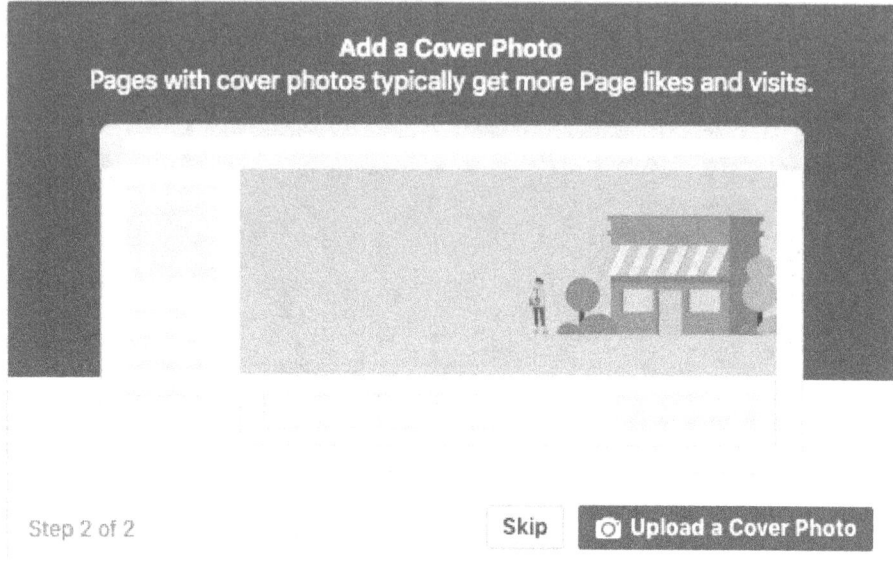

f. You now will be presented with your basic Business Facebook page. From here you should get used to the different items on the page and finish up the page by creating a short description, creating a username and other personalization's that fit your business that makes the page appealing to your future customers.

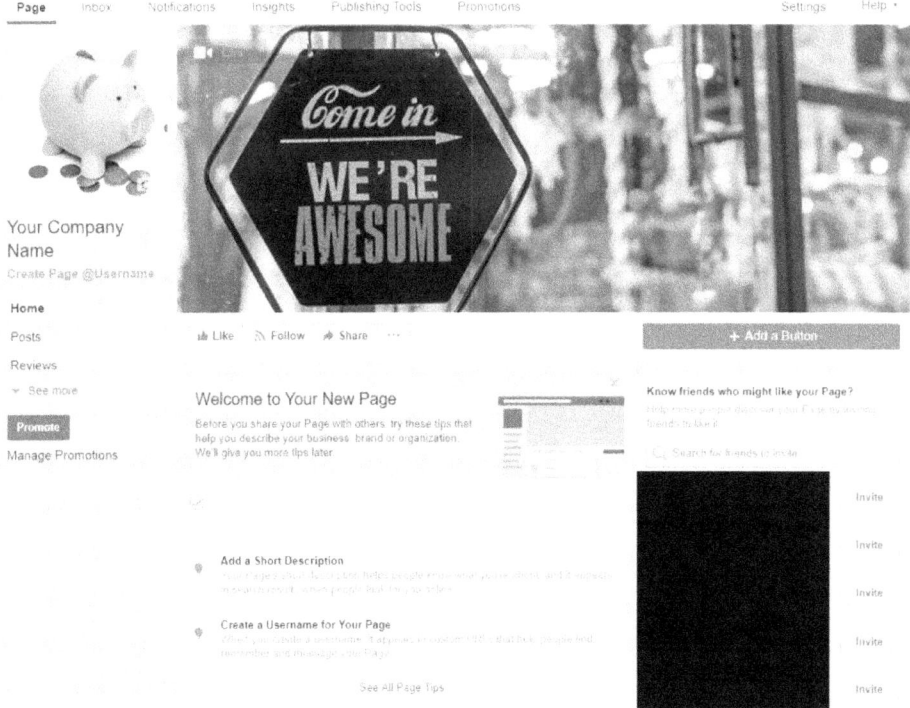

2. Setup your Facebook Ad Account

   a. Go to https://facebook.com/ads/manager and bookmark this link because this is your Facebook Ad

Manager dashboard that you will be working from often.

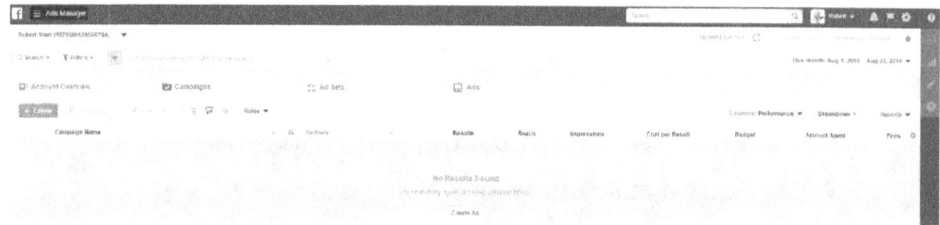

b. Click the drop down to the left of Ads Manager on the top left of the banner. We need to configure some basic items before actually creating ads so first choose Settings.

c. Ad Accounts -   Every account is assigned an Ad Account ID from Facebook that you can't change. Ad Account Name: I recommend changing this to something that represents what the ads are selling. When and if you create multiple Ad Accounts it will be easier to remember what those ads are. Time Zone: Changing the Time Zone will cause a message to pop up telling you that a new ad account will be created. Unless you are concerned about your reports or ads being based on Pacific Time Zone, I wouldn't change it as a beginner. Advertising Purposes: Of course, you are buying ads for business purposes so don't change this. Business Name: Fill in the name of your business. Business Address: Fill in the address for your business. Business Country: Select the country youare located. Tax ID Number: Enter your Tax ID Number. Ad Agency: Assuming you are just beginning and doing this only for your business, leave the default of No, I am not an agency buying ads on behalf of an advertiser. Remember to click Save Changes.

I am not going to touch on Attribution or Ad Account Roles at this time as these are advanced functions and don't need configuration in order to create your first ad.

d. Payment Settings – Click on Add Payment Method

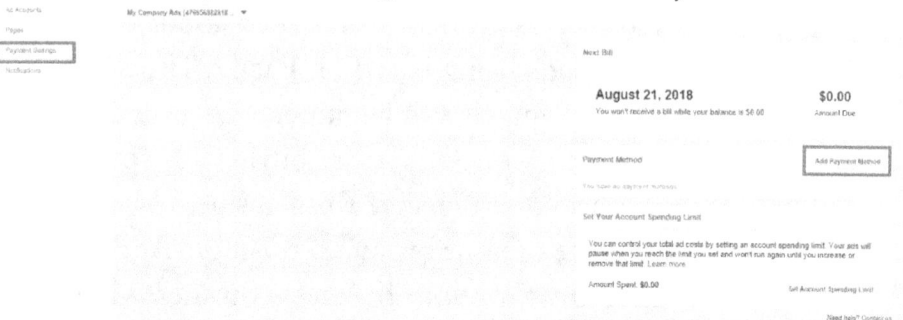

Facebook advertising is inexpensive but they aren't going to give it to you for free so fill in your method of payment. You have to use a credit/debit card, PayPal or add your bank account. I would use a credit card for billing reasons, tax purposes and security. Although, Facebook is secure, you wouldn't want someone being able to pull money directly out of your bank account. Credit cards also offer an easy way to report advertising costs which are tax deductible (see your accountant).

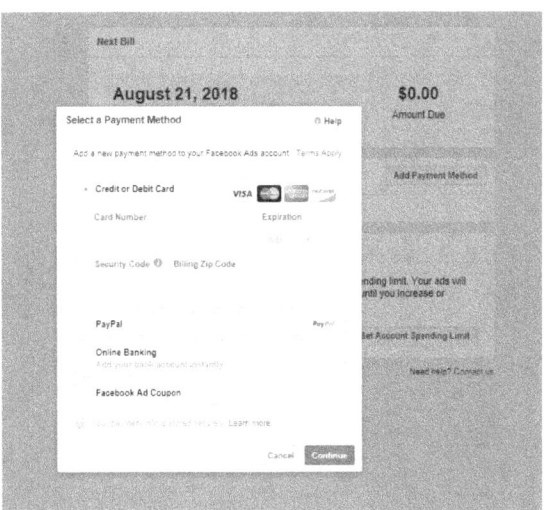

There is no need to change your Set Account Spending Limit to shut off your ads when a specific amount has been spent. You can control this when you create your ad and I would recommend you understand how much your ad(s) are spending from the actual ad form then from setting an Account Spending Limit.

e. Notifications – The only notification that I would change would be to turn on Ad Notifications on Messenger. I like to know when an ad is approved via my phone (must have messenger installed) if I'm not at my computer.

All Ad Account Notifications

All Email & Facebook Notifications
Only turn this off if you don't want to receive any notifications about your ad set performance, budget schedule and more.

Ad Email Notifications

The Facebook Ads Team sends you email notifications and marketing updates about your ad accounts to keep you informed. Even if you turn off all notifications, we may sometimes send you important updates about your ad account.

To change notification settings for other ad accounts, you'll need to update each ad account separately. If you've added ad accounts to Business Manager, you'll manage email settings for those accounts there.

Facebook will email you at **robertstarr10812@gmail.com** (Change this email)

Choose which notifications you want to receive

✓ **Payment completed**
An email notification any time your payment method is charged. This notification cannot be turned off.

✓ **Newsletter and product updates**
Periodic emails from Facebook with useful information about new advertising features, optimization tips, policy updates, and other news.

✓ **Ads summaries**
Weekly emails that list ad results and their schedules. Each email contains links to view those details and make changes in Ads Manager.

✓ **Ad creation reminder**
An email reminding you about an ad you didn't finish creating.

✓ **Ad review decisions**
Emails containing approval and disapproval information for ads submitted.

✓ **Dynamic ads alerts**
An email whenever there's an issue with your dynamic ads account.

✓ **Test and study updates**
Emails containing reports and updates about ad set split tests.

Ad Notifications on Facebook

Control which notifications you receive about your ads account.

✓ Ad approved

✓ Ad not approved

✓ Account settled

✓ Money added to balance

✓ Account out of money

✓ Account with low balance

✓ Payment completed

✓ Test and study updates

Ad Notifications on Messenger

Control notifications you receive about your ads in Messenger.

Ad updates, guidance and suggestions

Congratulations! You have successfully set up your Business Facebook Page and your Facebook Ads Manager. As promised it should not have taken you very long and was a painless process. The next module will help you create your first Facebook ad.

Module 2 Creating a Basic Facebook Ad

This module will assist you in creating your first basic Facebook Ad. Before we open Facebook Ads Manager and start creating the ad, it is always best to do some preliminary work of preparing for the ad. The reason so many people are unsuccessful with their Facebook ads is because they don't put any thought in ensuring each aspect of the ad is presented in the best way for the best results. Facebook studies show that you have only 8 seconds to grab someone's attention and get them to click on your ad. So, let's look at the parts of a Facebook ad and then map out what you will need for each part. I am going to utilize a Facebook Desktop Newsfeed Ad for illustration purposes because it presents the most information.

TEXT

The most important part of a Facebook Ad is the text. The picture may attract their initial attention but the quality of the text will determine whether someone will click on the ad or not and arrive at your landing page. It is always best to begin an ad with a question, specifically a question that identifies someone's pain. Facebook ads have the same principals as any print ad, radio or television commercial. They identify a pain someone is having first and then presents a solution on how you are going to remedy that pain. For instance, Glad garbage bag commercials show first how much garbage stinks and other bags tear easily causing the stinky garbage to spill all over the floor. Then during the second half of the commercial they demonstrate how their bag stretches, doesn't rip and keeps in all of the odor.

So, for the sample ad above, the picture may draw someone's attention to the beauty of the surroundings but it doesn't do anything more than that. The text begins by asking, Are you in a need of a vacation? And my guess is that everyone reading that line will say, YES. Another question follows that leads the reader to answer yes as well. So now we have the reader already saying yes to the pain we have identified.

Next, we are going to offer a remedy to the pain of needing a vacation and needing to disconnect, You can at this remote gem. We offer a lot of actionable words telling the reader that they can sleep, can leave, can re-energize. The reader now feels as though this is something they would be interested in, which leads to the next part of the text.

The reader now needs to be instructed on what to do and give them a sense of urgency on why they need to act now. In this case we state, Take advantage (the action) of our once a year promotion. (the urgency to act now). Other good options are to tell the reader exactly how to take action such as, Take action now by clicking on Learn More for our once a year promotion.

Remember that the text portion of the ad is just like a mini commercial and should not be any longer than necessary. The ad used as an example has all of that text appearing on desktop /

laptop screens but you need to take in consideration that mobile devices will have the text cutoff after a certain length and it will require them to manually click on the text to read the rest of it. Most readers will not take the time to read the whole text portion of the ad on a mobile device unless the first part of the text has really intrigued them. Until you get comfortable with the basics of Facebook ads, I wouldn't worry too much about what a mobile device sees but just keep that in the back of your mind when creating the ad.

Finally, the text should flow and make sense but unlike in the past, grammar and punctuation rules don't need to be adhered to as strictly. You only have a limited time and space to get someone to read your ad and then click to your landing page. Don't be concerned about all the individuals that will say otherwise because if texting, Facebook post responses, and other social media platforms have shown anything, people have become accepting to speaking differently online and social media.

IMAGE

Next piece in the ad is the actual picture that everyone will see initially. You can run slideshows and videos as well in this area but to get started for your first Facebook Ads, just stick with a single static image. Your picture should be related to what you are advertising as a rule of thumb. Types of images that work best for Facebook Ads are: Faces of smiling happy people, children and pets, images that use a color that contrasts with Facebook's color scheme so that your image stands out and showing a solid value such as FREE. Shock value or off the wall pictures work sometimes but I would stay clear of those until you have become more experienced in your Facebook Ad creations.

Facebook has their guidelines concerning pictures in ads and if they aren't followed, Facebook will suppress the ad from running to its' fullest or even not at all. The image needs to be 1200x628 pixels and contain as few words as possible. Facebook believes that people are deterred by images with an excessive amount of text so they have limited it to 20% of the image. You can create images with more than 20% text overlaid on the image but Facebook will warn you that your ad will not run as much as you hope or not at all. Facebook has created a free tool to help determine if your image meets their guidelines concerning text. You can find it at

https://www.facebook.com/ads/tools/text_overlay .

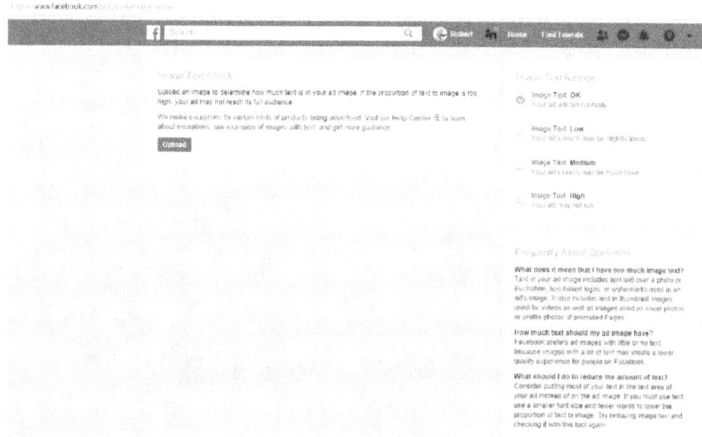

HEADLINE

Your headline is just like the headline of a newspaper article or a Google search result. It needs to draw the reader in so that they want to learn more but at the same time set the tone for what the reader will see in the ad and on your landing page. Nobody wants to be deceived or tricked into clicking an exciting ad only to be offered something totally unrelated. It is all about a relationship throughout the process that will make the reader comfortable and trust you to the point that they purchase your product. There are tons of opinions and trainings on creating a headline that works best. I have found that the headline that works best is the one that is to the point, factual and promises something that the reader will want. You will not get it right the first time necessarily but with trial and error and testing you will find the one that works the best for what you are offering.

Facebook guidelines concerning headlines is that it can't exceed 40 characters. The typical headline is only 5 words long. This will help those of you that tend to be long winded. Remember headlines are meant to draw someone's attention to read more not give all of the story.

LINK DESCRIPTION

The link description is your chance to tell people what to expect when they click on your ad and how to do it. Don't be afraid to tell people to click on the Call to Action button, because you will be amazed how many times I've had people ask what they needed to do to take advantage of an offer. Facebook suggests that the link description not be more than 30 characters but I believe in taking advantage of the space given in this area. Longer link descriptions will be cutoff on mobile devices so the first part of the description needs to contain the most important part but desktop / laptop users will be able to see longer descriptions.

One trick I've learned is to ask the current reader of my ad in the link description to like and share the ad with their family and friends. If they are interested in what is being offered there is a good chance that their family and friends will have similar interest and tastes. This line of text may not work for your ads but again testing and trial and error will lead you to the best link description.

AUDIENCE

You are probably thinking wait, I don't see audience listed in the sample ad. But it is a very important piece of your ad that you need to think about before creating the ad in the Facebook Ads Manager. Who is your customer? What demographics do you need to target? Facebook makes it very simple to target the people with your ads but first you have to have a starting point. Facebook targeting is broken down into overall groups that are then broken down into subsets. The main groups are demographics, location, interests and behaviors. There are other more advanced methods to target potential customers with your ad but we will start with beginning steps first.

Using the sample ad, you might want to target people that need a vacation, who live in the North with no beaches and it snows, and most likely has the financial means to go to an exotic location as shown. When we actually start creating the ad in Facebook Ad Manager, you will see where this information is located and configured. At least get your mind thinking about these items and your target audience that will buy your product before you create you ad.

Take time to outline and create some ads that you think will work for what you are advertising. Remember you are just starting out and you aren't going to hit a home run the first time out and you shouldn't copy and paste from other Facebook ads. If you just want a cookie cutter ad then you will not be successful, so spend the time to think out each part of the ad before hand. After you have outlined on paper and have your image ready, you will be ready to move onto the next step and get your hands dirty actually creating the ad in Facebook Ads Manager.

So, let's open your Facebook Ads Manager by going to https://facebook.com/ads/manager which you hopefully have bookmarked from earlier, because you will be spending a lot of time there.

1. Click on Create

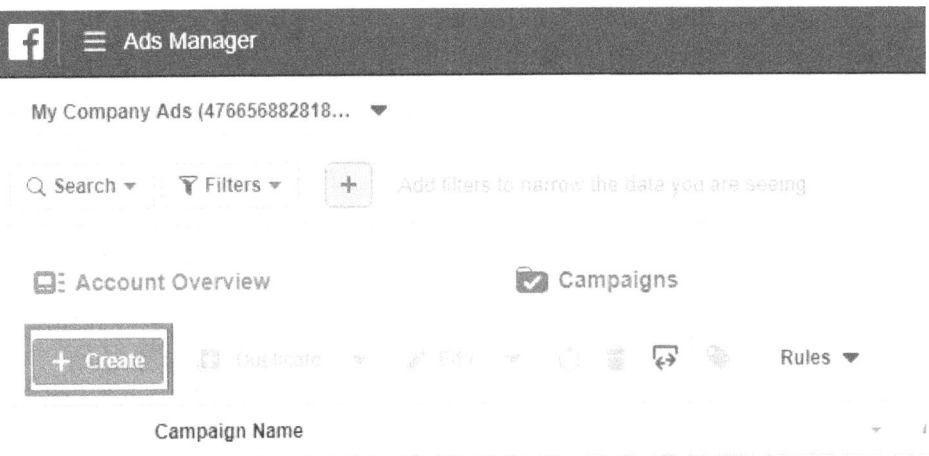

2. If you see the following screen, choose Select Guided Creation

How do you want to create ad campaigns?

Create complete campaigns
Fill in all of the details now and end up with completed drafts that are ready to run

Create campaign shells
Set up your campaign structure and fill in the details for your ad sets and ads later

Select Guided Creation

Select Quick Creation

Having trouble selecting a creation method?

3. The next screen will offer you a chance to pick your marketing objective. Since you are just starting out let's pick Traffic. The Traffic objective will direct the most amount of traffic to your landing page and is a good place to start. Facebook with all of its data is able to place your ad in front of the best people possible to get your desired result for example if you wanted a lot of people to view your video ad they would show your ad more often to those who are known to watch videos the most. The other objectives and how to utilize them the best will be covered

in a later module. In the Campaign Name box, give your new ad campaign a name by creating a name that immediately tells you what the campaign is. You want to create a naming convention that works for your business. You will be glad you did when you start creating multiple campaigns.

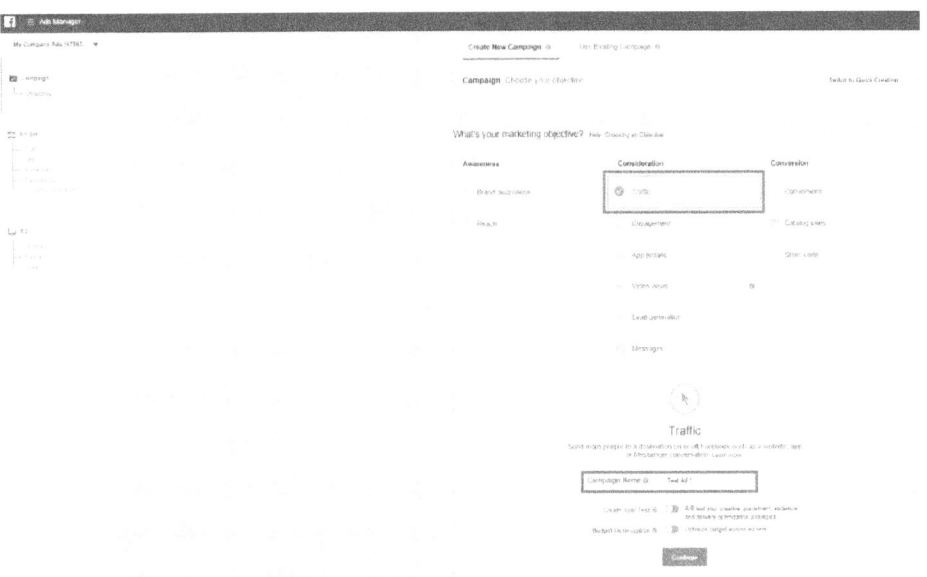

4. Now we start using some of our pre-planning on the next page. In this module we are going to only deal with creating one Ad Set under your campaign. Facebook allows for multiple Ad Sets to be created under a Campaign which is ideal for A/B testing in order to find the most optimum producing Ad Set. Ad Sets are where you will configure who the audience is, where the ad is placed within the Facebook world and budget & scheduling. I'll will cover each section of this page separately.

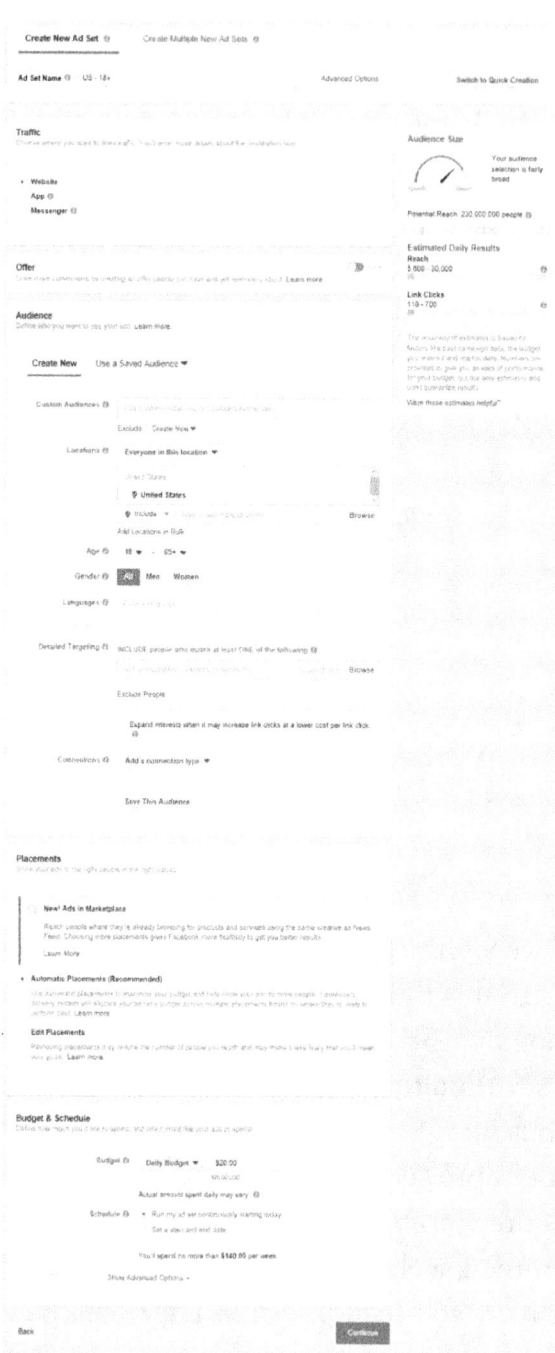

5. Create an Ad Set Name and type it into the designated line. Later, when you start doing more advanced configuring with multiple ad sets for testing, you will want to ensure to create a naming convention that is immediately recognizable of what you were testing.

Create New Ad Set   Create Multiple New Ad Sets

Ad Set Name   Facebook Test Ad

6. Next on this page is the Audience section where you will tell Facebook who to target and show your ads to. You need to know who your audience is for your product or service. If you don't, you could end up spending a lot of money displaying your ad to people who have zero interest. I'm going to break down each subsection of this area in order to give you as much detailed information as possible and you get the best results.
    a. Create New – For the purpose of this module and setting up your first Audience, we will start with creating a new Audience.
    b. Potential Reach – In the right column, the potential reach will display the potential reach your ad will have before you start pinpointing your targeted audience. By default, if you are in the US, it will start currently at 230,000,000 people. This number

will start to decrease as you configure your audience. The ideal number will vary depending on what your ad objective is and where your targeted best customers are located.

c. Estimated Daily Results Reach - Facebook with all of their data and algorithms gives an estimated number of how many people have the potential to view your ad based on the Potential Reach and your daily budget.

d. Link Clicks – Taking it a step further Facebook will give you an estimated amount of people that they think will actually click on the ad.

e. Custom Audience – A very useful tool for remarketing and finding new potential leads for your ads but this will be covered in later modules.

f. Locations – This is where you will tell Facebook where in the USA or world to display your ads. If you pick a specific city, Facebook defaults to a 25 mile radius but you can adjust that from 1 mile to 50 mile radius. The larger the area, the more people who will be in the Audience bucket and will potentially view your ad. As you adjust the location section, you will notice that the Potential Reach number will change as well.

g. Age – The default age range that Facebook will display your ad to is 18 to 65+. You will need to adjust the range based on knowing who your best audience would be for your product or service. As you run more ads and view Facebook's reports, you will be able to focus this in to the optimum group that is responding to your ads and buying.

h. Gender – The default is All and unless you are offering something that is specific to either Men or Women, there is no need to change this. Although, you may determine after checking the reports that Women are responding way better to a certain ad and then it may be conducive to adjusting this section.

i. Languages – This section gives you the opportunity to target a demographic that speaks a particular language who are your target audience.

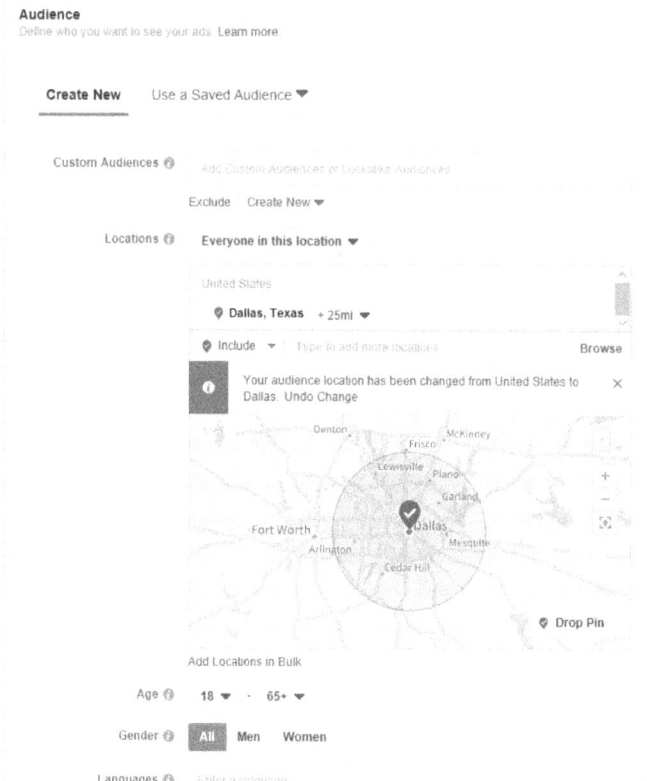
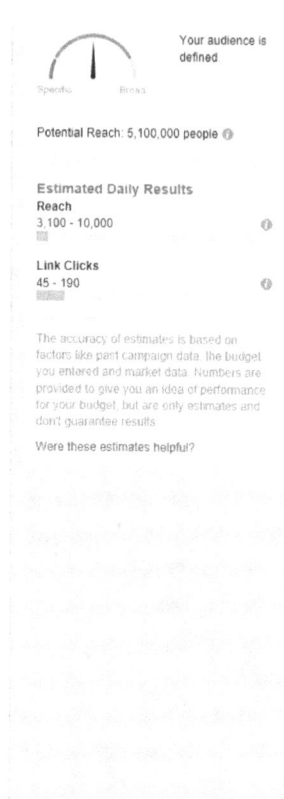

j. Detailed Targeting – This is where you can really start to narrow down the target audience that will be displayed your ad. You obviously don't want to be spending money displaying your ad for a beach vacation to people who only like to snow ski on vacation. You will find that Facebook has 3 categories in this section, Interests, Behaviors and Demographics and the list is vast. Just start typing a keyword such as Vacations into the line and Facebook will start bringing up items that are related. Be as specific as possible but if after typing something and nothing is displayed then Facebook doesn't have any potential people in that category. If you hover your mouse over a specific item, a popup will appear that displays the total number of people on Facebook that are associated with that item, the actual category and a description of the category. This becomes useful to find future targeted audiences and to see how many people in the Location you chose earlier that are interested in that specific item. Too many people in the potential reach and you might decide it best to find a more specific Interest, Behavior or Job Title or too few and you might want to add another topic to the list. The key is to find and target the best group of people that will be interested in your ad and then will take action.

Facebook also assists you in finding audiences that are similar to the audience you added. Just click on Suggestions after an item or two and Facebook will list items that you may never have thought of such as Frequent Travelers or Adventure travel. Facebook wants you to succeed with your ads and this is one area they offer a great tool to help you find a targeted audience that will be most interested in your ads and ultimately click to your landing page where they will take action. If you click on Browse, a drop down will appear which will give you the opportunity to manually click through all the sub-categories available in Detailed Targeting. This method is time consuming but I would recommend you take a look at it at least once.

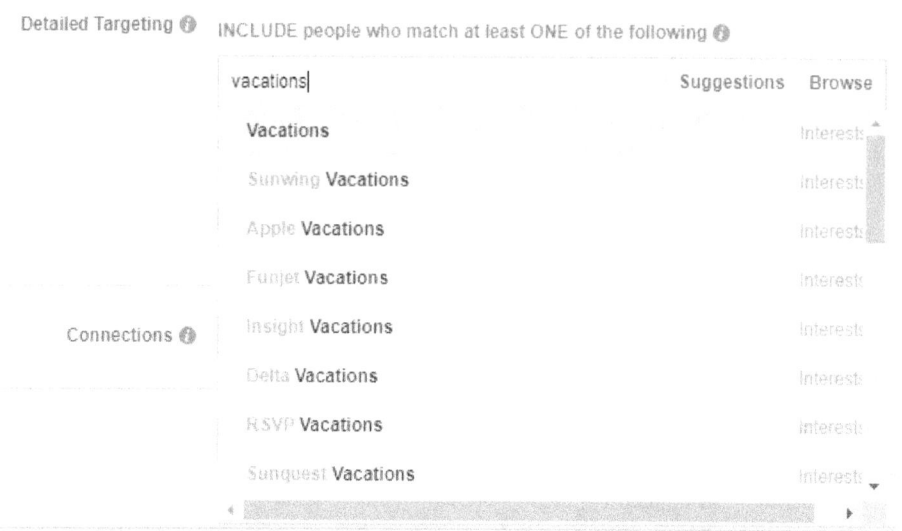

This section may take some trial and error and creating multiple ad sets with different Audiences but it will assist you in finding the right targeted audience. To start though, I would just stick to one ad set until you are comfortable with creating a Facebook ad and how to understand the stats and reports which are covered in a future module.

7. Now that we have told Facebook where in the world we want our ad displayed and who to display it to, we need to tell them where in the Facebook domain to display the ad. There are two initial options under Placements; Automatic Placements and Edit Placements. Facebook recommends the Automatic Placement because they say they can place your ads more efficiently for your budget. Facebook is continually updating their available data and algorithms and the Automatic Placement may be getting better at what is says it does but most Facebook marketers will tell you that they would rather control where their ad is being placed. As a beginner it is always best to understand each placement anyway so that you can find what works best for you. So, let's go ahead and choose Edit Placements instead.

Placements
Show your ads to the right people in the right places

 New! Ads in Marketplace
Reach people where they're already browsing for products and services using the same creative as News Feed. Choosing more placements gives Facebook more flexibility to get you better results.
Learn More

- **Automatic Placements (Recommended)**
Use automatic placements to maximize your budget and help show your ads to more people. Facebook's delivery system will allocate your ad set's budget across multiple placements based on where they're likely to perform best. Learn more

Edit Placements
Removing placements may reduce the number of people you reach and may make it less likely that you'll meet your goals. Learn more.

After clicking on Edit Placements, the window will expand and show all the platforms that are available for displaying your ad. First are Device Types which I recommend you don't change from the default of All Devices. Next are all the platforms and as you hover your mouse over each platform location a preview pops up to the right that shows what it looks like. Just like every piece of Facebook ads that we have discussed so far, this is all customizable and you may benefit from testing different placements to achieve your best result.

   a. Facebook – Includes all the usual locations that you are accustomed to seeing ads on Facebook. If a particular location is not available for your traffic objective, Facebook won't have it checked or let you check it.
   b. Instagram – For this beginning module of creating your first Facebook ad, go ahead and uncheck Instagram. Instagram has its' own configuration requirements that are dealt with in a future module.
   c. Audience Network – The audience network has been greatly improved and it is the placement of your ad off of Facebook with other apps and mobile websites. This allows you to target your audience with the same ads and the more eyes that see your ad the better.
   d. Messenger – Facebook Messenger is a very popular app and is the second most widely used messenger app behind WhatsApp. Again, the more eyes that see your ad typically the better.

There is nothing else in this section that you need to change or configure.

- **Edit Placements**
  Removing placements may reduce the number of people you reach and may make it less likely that you'll meet your goals. Learn more.

  Device Types

  All Devices (Recommended) ▼

  Asset Customization ⓘ
  Select all placements that support asset customization

  Platforms

  ▼ Facebook —
      Feeds ✓
      Instant Articles ✓
      In-Stream Videos
      Right Column ✓
      Suggested Videos
      Marketplace ✓
      Stories

  ▼ Instagram ✓
      Feed ✓
      Stories ✓

  ▼ Audience Network ✓
      Native, Banner and Interstitial ✓
      In-Stream Videos
      Rewarded Videos ✓

  ▼ Messenger ✓
      Inbox ✓
      Sponsored Messages

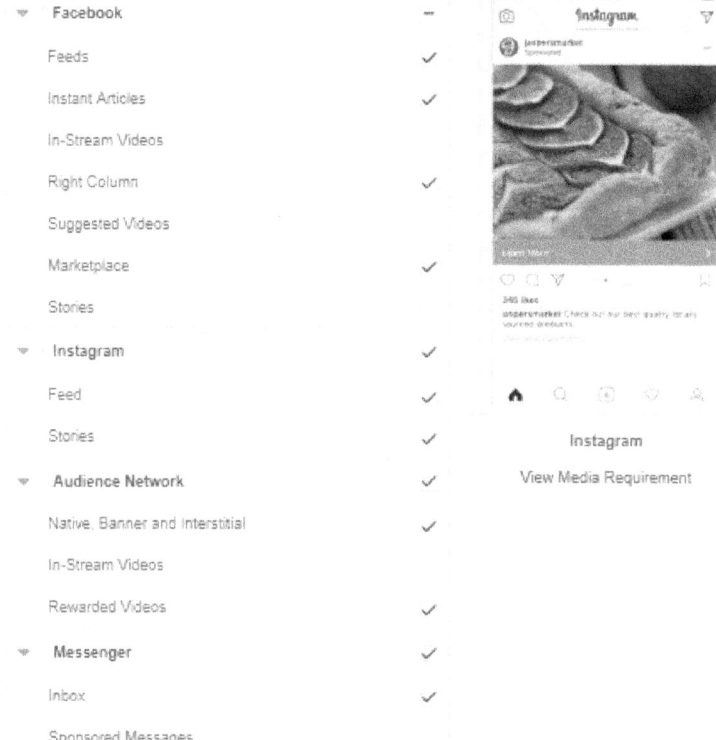

Instagram
View Media Requirement

  Specific Mobile Devices & Operating Systems

  All Mobile Devices ▼

      Only when connected to Wi-Fi

  Exclude Content and Publishers
  Available for Audience Network, Instant Articles and In-Stream Videos.

  Apply Block Lists ⓘ

8. Budget and Schedule are next up. Here you will define how much you want to spend on your ad and the time schedule. You can start with a budget as little as $20 a day, while there are marketers spending hundreds a day on just one ad. I recommend you start low until you dial in the perfect ad and then ramp up your spending to get more results. The more money you spend a day the higher your Estimated Daily Results Reach and Link Clinks will be. Spending more money isn't always the best option or solution to resolving any issues of a lack of people clicking on your ad. In fact, depending on the audience size, I've witnessed where there can be a tipping point where spending more money doesn't result in more clicks and the cost to the run the ad increases. In a later module, learning to understand the Facebook Stats and Reporting will assist you in finding that sweet spot for spending on any particular ad.

    You can choose between Daily Budget or Lifetime Budget. Some people may only have a specific amount of money that they can spend so they think they should pick Lifetime Budget. You still have to change the schedule to tell Facebook what timeframe to run the ad and they then take your budget and divide it by the amount of days you choose to run your ad. It limits you from adjusting your spend based on results by choosing that. I would always recommend choosing Daily Budget.

    Now is the time to decide how much you want to spend per day based on your allotted total budget. Just take the amount you have to spend and divide how many days you want to run the ad. As your ad is running you may find certain days don't produce as well as others, so you can manually lower the daily spend for that day and then add the left over money to days that perform better. To start for your first ad, just be concerned about what your daily spend will be for the ad.

Next, you need to schedule your ad. You can choose Run my ad set continuously starting today or Set a start and end date. I wouldn't use the first option for a couple of reasons; as a beginner setting an ad and forgetting it is too much temptation to never checking the results and tweaking the ad as necessary and you may find yourself quickly over budget with poorly producing ads if you tell Facebook to just keep displaying my ad. Facebook wants you to succeed with your ads and gives you all the tools to accomplish that but they are also a business and won't mind taking your money either. Even if you are a more seasoned Facebook marketer with Evergreen ads, I would always set a start and end date for an ad. This forces you to monitor your ads and to make changes if necessary, even your best ad that has been running like clockwork for months has the potential to falter due to Facebook changes, a change in public interest for a subject or item or a competitor that tweaked their ad to work better than yours.

If you choose Run my ad set continuously, Facebook will display on a schedule based on the most you will pay per week on your ad. Choosing and setting a set start and end date, Facebook will display how many days your ad will run and the most you will spend on that ad at the end of the set number of days. This is a good check and balance to ensure you aren't spending more than what your allocated budget is for your ad.

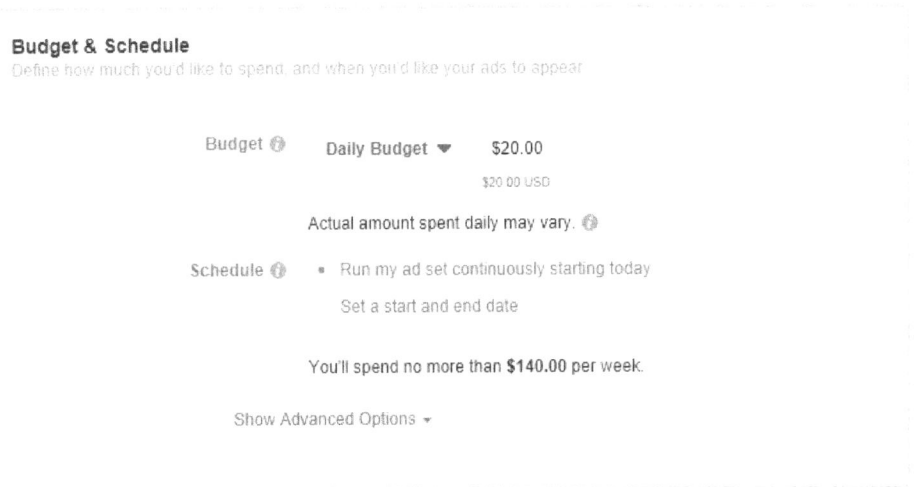

Facebook doesn't require you to click on Show Advanced Options but this section should be automatically displayed and even as a beginner you should be reviewing this section so be sure to click Show Advanced Options.

    a. Optimization for Ad Delivery – When you click on the drop-down arrow that says Link Clicks you will see 4 different options for ad delivery.

Link Clinks is the default option and for a good reason. It works best for almost everyone's advertising goals of getting people to click on the ad to get to your landing page and it is the lowest cost.

Landing Page Views. The idea behind this is Facebook believes using that option they will be able to optimize your ad to be displayed to people who are patient enough for your landing page to load versus those who close your landing page because it loaded too slowly. Developing a landing page is a whole different training but if your landing page is loading too slowly then it needs to be optimized to do so.

Impressions will deliver your ad to as many people as Facebook can and you will pay for each time they display your ad. This works if you are doing a product launch and you want to get the word out about your new product or service and you aren't worried about how many people actually arrive at your landing page. But be warned, it is also the most expensive option.

Daily Unique Reach limits your ads to being displayed only once per day to any particular person. Statistics show that people need to see or hear something about 7 times before they take action. So only displaying an ad once a day to a person probably isn't going to have great results.

b. Bid Strategy – You can check this if you don't want Facebook to bid more than a certain amount to display your ad but the cost of advertising is so cheap on Facebook there is no need to check this.

c. When You Get Charged – The default is Impressions but as mentioned in the Optimization for Ad Delivery section this is the most expensive way to run your ads. Facebook will gladly collect the fees for charging you for impressions so I would click on More Options and choose Link Click (CPC). Note: If this is your first Facebook ad, you can't change to Link Click until you have spent $10 using Impressions. Just remember to change it to Link Click as soon as possible.

d. Ad Scheduling – when just starting out with Facebook ads I would leave the default of Run ads all the time. As you become more experience and understand the stats and reports from your ads, you may choose to change to Run ads on a schedule. With this option you will be able to stop or reduce your ads during the time of day that aren't producing results. Note: Run ads on a schedule is only available if you use Lifetime Budgets which was discussed early.

e. Delivery Type – The default is Standard and you should just leave it that way. Choosing Accelerated spends your budget faster and gets you faster results according to Facebook. This is counterintuitive though to how Facebook ads work. Facebook spends about 24 hours learning what is the best way overall to display your ad and by rushing them for results you are giving up the power of Facebook's algorithms.

9. You probably didn't believe you would ever get through the Ad Set section of creating a new ad but congratulations you have made it. Click on Continue at the bottom of the page to continue to the last stage and submit the copy and image you created when pre-planning. We will go through this section piece by piece as well to ensure you understand all the different options.

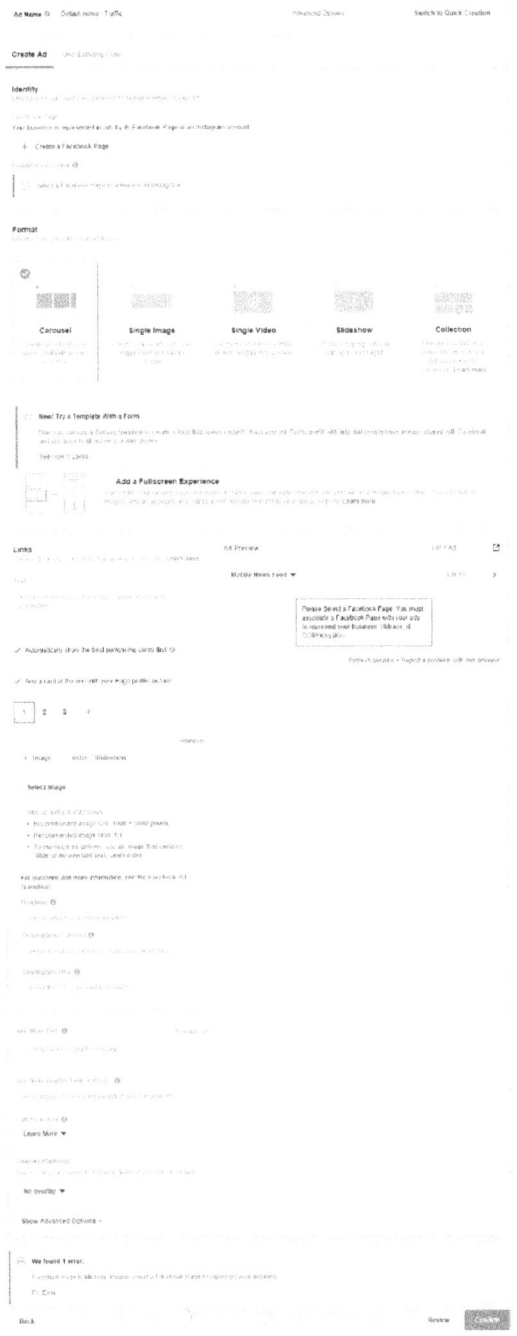

10. The first thing you want to do is to enter an Ad Name at the top and just like the Campaign Name and Ad Set Name, you want to create a naming convention for your ads so that you can tell what the ad is. Almost everyone will leave Create Ad as default because Use Existing Post is a more advanced feature to be left for another time. Next is identity which should show your Facebook Business Page that you created in Module 1. Instagram Account should be blank for now even if you have an Instagram page. Attaching your Instagram page and configuring ads for it will be covered in another module. Starting out just concern yourself with learning what is required for Facebook ads.

11. Next, we come to the format section which includes 5 options which have descriptions under each: Carousel, Single Image, Single Video, Slideshow, Collection. Starting out we will only concern ourselves with the Single Image option so click on that option.

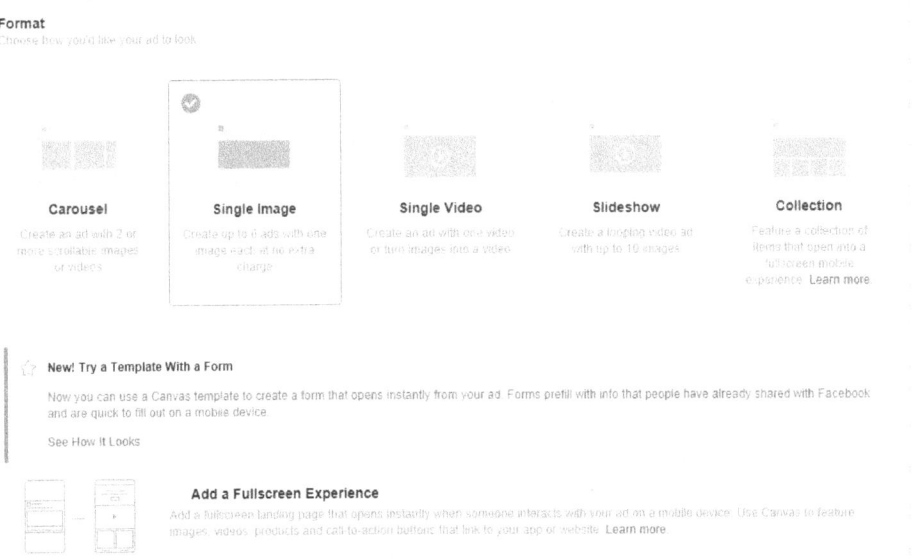

12. Moving down the page is Images. Click on Upload Images, locate the image you created during pre-planning that is 1200x628 pixels and upload it. When it is done loading the picture will appear in two places, right in the images section and in the Ad Preview window just to the right and below this section. The Image area also has the option to browse your library which are all the images you have previously used for ads and Free Stock Images. It is not recommended to use stock images unless you alter them because they are images that everyone and anyone can use

and they won't make your ad stand out among all the others.

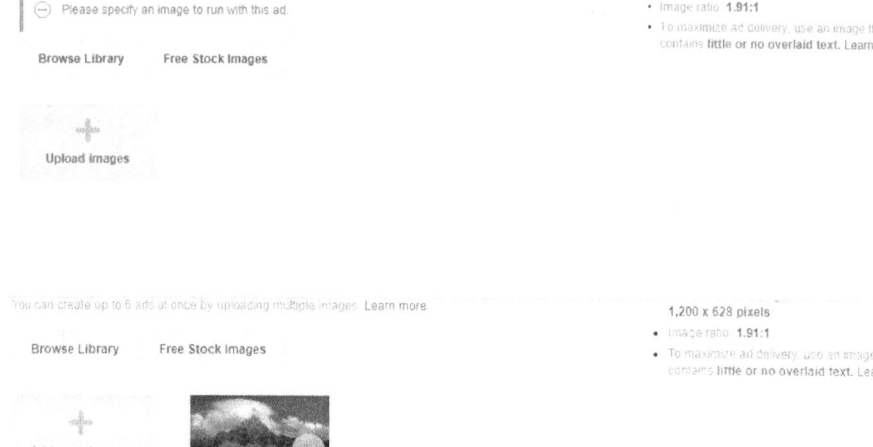

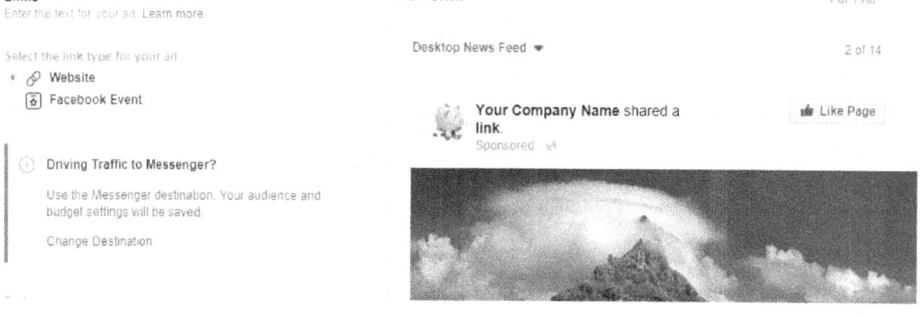

13. You will now enter the text from your pre-planning in the Text box. As you type the text it will appear in the preview screen. If you want to see how your text will appear in the different platforms, all you need to do is click on the dropdown at the top of preview screen or click the arrows to the right of the dropdown box. Next enter the URL for the landing page you are directing everyone to. This will appear in the preview screen below the image. Then take the Headline you created from your pre-planning and enter it into the Headline box. You can change the Call To Action by clicking on the dropdown arrow next to Learn More. Learn More is the #1 call to action utilized in Facebook ads but you can test other call to actions as you become accustomed to doing Facebook ads. Finally, enter your text from you pre-planning into the News Feed Link Description. This is the last item that you need to configure for your first Facebook ad. Other configurations listed on the page will be covered in later modules.

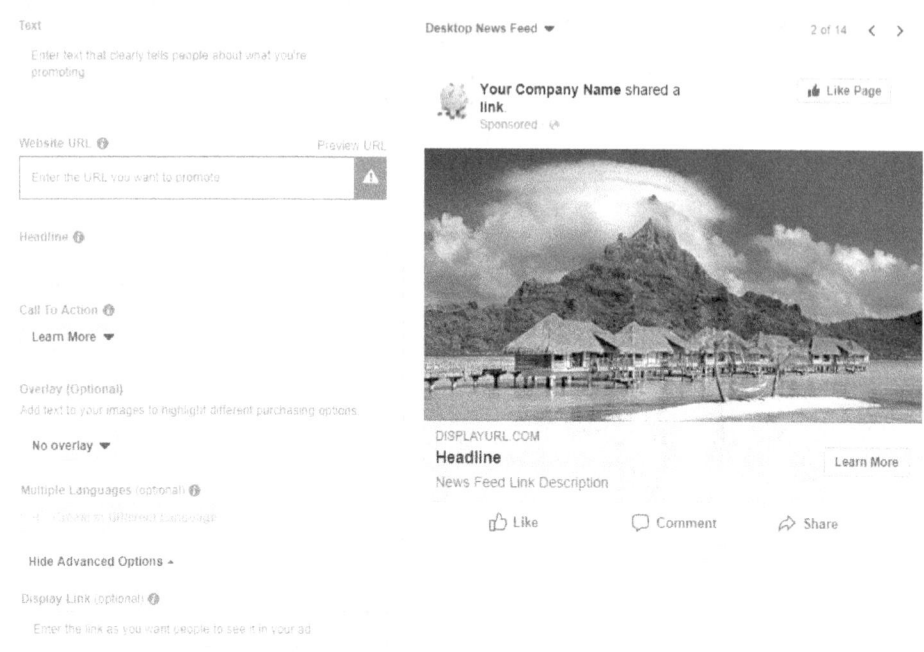

Review your ad in the preview screen ensuring you don't have any typos. You want to get comments from people who view or ad but trust me, all it takes is one typo to distract from your message and for people to fill your comments pointing out your typo. After you are satisfied with your ad, hit Confirm and your ad will be published.

Congratulations, after Facebook reviews and approves your ad, it will start to be displayed to your targeted audience for the timeframe you configured. You have successfully created your first ad, people are beginning to view your ad and arriving at your landing page. Tweaking your ad or creating new ads for A/B testing can begin but how do you know if your ad is producing the results expected for the lowest cost possible. Facebook gives you all the data you will need to analyze your running ads. Module 3 will cover understanding Facebook ad stats and reporting.

Module 3 Facebook Ad Reports

You have successfully created your first Facebook ad but how do you tell if it is producing positive results? Facebook gives you all the tools to analyze the data from your ad and sometimes they give too much data. It can be overwhelming sometimes viewing all of the data available so I will go through all different data points available and recommend which ones are the most important. Note: There are industry typical averages for certain data points. Not every industry will have same cost results and at the end I will point you to a website to compare your results with others in the same industry. I will give samples from a couple of different products/industries in this module to illustrate differences.

I'm going to go through and explain what each data set is and then later in this module I will go more in depth concerning what are good results and how to read the data so that you can determine what ads are working and which ones need to be tweaked or turned off. Facebook is constantly updating their system so what you see here may not be the standard view 6 months from now.

1. The Facebook Ads Manager screen is standard for everyone when they first open it but it is customizable to your needs. The data for your campaigns is shown first but as we progress through the reports, you can switch to Ad Sets and Ads as well. First, we will work though the overall big picture of your campaigns.

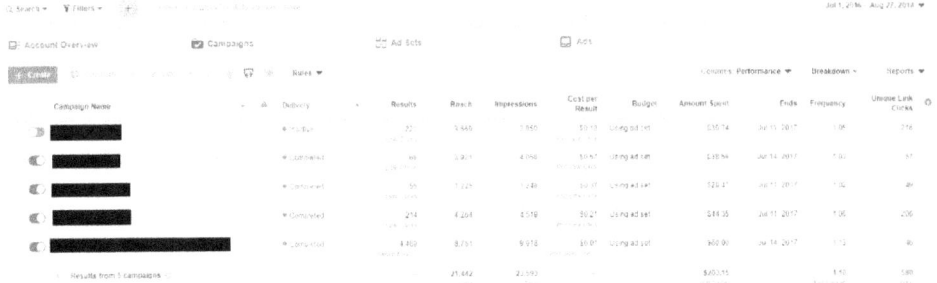

a. Date Range - In the top right corner is a date range with a dropdown arrow. By default, the date will be the current month but by clicking on the dropdown arrow you have the option of picking a custom date range using the calendars or picking from a list under Date Presets.

b. Columns – The default will display Performance but there is a dropdown arrow that permits you to choose other columns that will be displayed. You can also customize the columns that will be displayed when you open your Facebook Ads Manager. To start we will leave the default Performance for columns.

c. Breakdown – By utilizing this dropdown, you can breakdown your data in more ways than you probably ever imagined. You may find this useful later after you grasp the basics of reporting but I'm not going to cover it here.

d. Reports – With this dropdown you can export your report, create a custom report or share a link so that someone else can see the report.

e. Campaign Name – The campaigns that you create will be listed here. If the campaign is inactive, the switch to the left of the name will be grey and if the campaign is active or completed the switch will be blue. This switch gives you the ability to turn on or off campaigns as you see fit. I recommend checking this daily. There have been times, although not that often, where a campaign has turned off without me knowing it and for no reason.

f. Delivery - This column displays if a campaign is Active, Completed or Inactive.

g. Results – This column displays the total amount of Link Clinks or people who clicked on your campaign and then arrived at your landing page. If you have multiple ad sets then this total is the combination of all the ad sets associated with that particular campaign. This is different than how many unique link clicks there which is explained later.

h. Reach – This column displays the amount of people your ad was displayed to. So, for the first campaign in the example in this section, 3,669 people had the opportunity to view the campaign. If you have multiple ad sets then this total is the combination of all the ad sets associated with that particular campaign.

i. Impressions – This is how many times your ad was displayed. The reach was 3,669 but some of those people had the campaign displayed to them more than once. If you have multiple ad sets then this total is the combination of all the ad sets associated with that particular campaign.

j. Cost Per Result – This column displays the cost per click of someone clicking on your campaign and arriving on your landing page. Remember in Module 2 we set the way we wanted billed to Cost Per Click and this where we see the result of that. To calculate this number, you take the amount you spent divided by the link clicks. The obvious thing is that you want this number to be as low as possible. Later I will give a resource to check to see what is normal for your industry. Never do research to find out other's Cost per Click because you will be comparing apples to oranges when it comes to industry norms. If you have multiple ad sets then this total is the combination of all the ad sets associated with that particular campaign.

k. Budget – This column does not pertain to Campaigns but to Ad Sets

l. Amount Spent – This column will display how much money you have currently spent on your campaign and how much is expected to be spent.

m. Ends – This column displays when the campaign is set to end.

n. Frequency – This column displays the amount of times on average your campaign was displayed to one person.

o. Unique Link Clicks – This column displays how many unique people clicked on your campaign. The Results column was a total of Link Clicks because there are going to be people who see your ad multiple times and click on it every time. If you have multiple ad sets then this total is the combination of all the ad sets associated with that particular campaign.

2. Ad Sets – Go ahead and click on Ad Sets and you will notice that a similar page as Campaigns appears but these

are the Ad Sets you created and a few slight differences in the columns displayed. I will only go over the differences with this page.

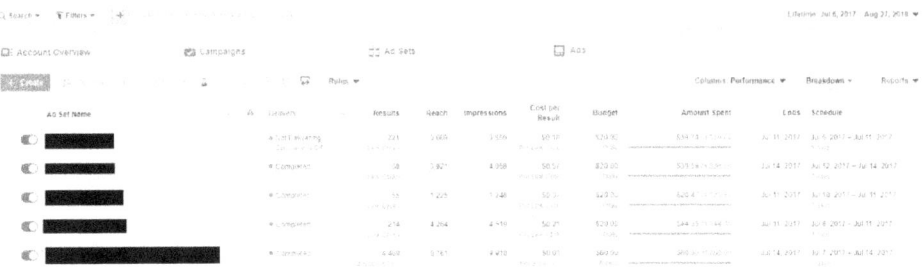

Instead of a Campaign Name column, there is an Ad Set Name column and there is the switch to turn on or off a single ad set. If you have a campaign with multiple ad sets for testing, you can analyze each ad set separately and turn off the one for the campaign that is underperforming.

The Results, Reach, Impressions, Cost per Result and End remain the same and are the data for that specific ad set.

The Budget column displays how much you have allocated to spend on each ad set.

The Schedule column displays the start and end date for that particular ad set.

3. Ads – When you click on Ads you will see a similar page as Campaigns and Ad Sets, only this data is related to the Ads people see.

This time the first column is labeled Ad Name which displays all of the ads that you have created. You will notice that besides the ad name there is also a thumbnail of graphic you utilized with the ad and the switch to turn on or off an ad is present. You can have multiple ads running per ad set for testing just like you could have multiple ad sets per campaign for testing. By analyzing this data you will be able to determine if a particular ad is underperforming and turn it off.

The Delivery, Results, Reach, Impressions, Cost per Result, Amount Spent and Ends columns all remain the same but are related to that specific ad.

The next column is the Relevance Score is important to pay attention to. The Relevance Score is a number between 1 – 10 that Facebook assigns to your ad based on how well your target audience is responding to your Facebook ad. Anything lower than a 6 is an indication that you need to change your image or copy in your ad. A Relevance Score isn't given until your ad has had 500 impressions.

Frequency displays an estimate of how many times your ad is displayed to a single person.

Unique Clicks is different than the Results column. Results show the total number of clicks your ad had but Unique Clicks displays how many people actually clicked your ad. If your ad is being displayed more than once per person and they click each time they see the ad then their multiple clicks raises the Results but all their clicks only count as 1 in the Unique Clicks column.

This covers the three basic screens for analyzing your Facebook advertising results. The Campaigns screen is the overall picture of what is happening with your advertising and may be the only screen you initially use if you have created only 1 Ad Set and 1 Ad per campaign to determine if your ad campaign is producing positive results. But, as you become more experienced with Facebook advertising you will find yourself checking the results from the Ad level first then working your way up to the overall picture of the Campaigns. Without a strong foundation which are your Ads, your Ad Sets and Campaigns won't produce the results you are looking for. So, let's take a look at the different data points and get a better idea of what a good result should look like.

Results may vary…. We have all seen this disclaimer and it is relevant when analyzing your Facebook advertising. What is a good result for one industry may be a poor result for another. While one advertiser is experienced and understands audience targeting, there will be another that struggles with audience targeting but is proficient at writing copy and ad graphics. The goal though is to learn where your results should be for your product / industry. I am going to start at the Ad level since it is the foundation for your Campaigns.

Your Ad is the first thing that a potential customer sees while spending time on Facebook so it needs to be inviting enough to cause the viewer to click on it and end up at your landing page. The first data point that Facebook provides to determine that is the Relevancy Score found on the Ads screen which was show earlier. The Relevance Score is an estimated determination by Facebook of how well your targeted audience is responding to your Ad. The scale is from 1 to 10 with 10 being the best score. Any score under 6 is considered a poor response from your targeted audience which means that certain elements of your Ad need to be revised. Lower Relevance Scores also will cost you more to run because Facebook will restrict their distribution but they will reward you with cheaper running ads that have a high Relevance Score. Remember your Relevance Score today may not be what it is tomorrow as Facebook is constantly running their analytics. So, be sure to monitor it often and update and edit your ads as necessary.

Typical ways to improve your Relevance Score are:

1. Targeting the best audience. You don't want to run ads directed at someone who would have no interest in your product. Be sure to pick the best groups of people and the more focused the group the better. In later modules, I'll discuss how to use the power of Facebook

to use your database of current customers and find more that are just like them.
2. Your ad should have value for the customer to click. Make sure those who see your ad see a clear value to leave Facebook and give you their time and attention on your landing page.
3. Make your copy about the customer and speak in the 1st person. Also include action words and create a sense of urgency. You want the reader to have a sense that there is a positive relationship already created between the two of you while at the same time making them have a sense that they have to act now or they will miss out. People inherently have FOMO – Fear Of Missing Out.
4. Ensuring that your copy and/or graphic are inline with your landing page. If your Ad promises something then you need to ensure when they get to your landing page that the first thing they see is what you promised. People do not like to be tricked into clicking on an Ad only to find something totally different presented to them.
5. Using the proper graphic. Pictures of smiling people have a tendency to create a more pleasant experience thus causing them to click on your ad more often. In addition, using colors that are contrasting to the Facebook color scheme is effective. You need to find ways to make your ad stand out from all of the other clutter on Facebook but be sure not to get too carried away with your color choices.

6. The sure way to increase your Relevance Score is the utilization of video instead of static graphics. Facebook studies show that video ads have an extremely better response rates versus a picture. When first starting out Facebook advertisers utilize pictures until they become more comfortable with the system but you should consider moving to video ads as soon as you become more comfortable with them.

The data point that people focus on most is how much is the Ad costing you to display to people on Facebook. The Cost per Result column will give you that information. The lower the Cost per Click or CPC the better for you and the more Ads that will be displayed on Facebook for your budget. You will see all kinds of numbers thrown around the internet for where your CPC should be but as mentioned earlier what is good for one product / industry may be bad for someone else and vice versa. Traditionally though your CPC I say should not go above $1.00 even though the Aug 2018 average is $1.72 CPC across all industries. I recommend checking the following website a couple of times a year to get updated analytics concerning the cost of running ads on Facebook because they break it all down by various categories including CPC per industry (https://www.wordstream.com/blog/ws/2017/02/28/facebook-advertising-benchmarks). Just with Relevance Score, video ads typically have the best results and the lowest CPC. When starting out don't get frustrated that the results aren't matching your expectations. It takes a while to dial in what targeted audience, copy and graphics work the best for your product. Just like the Relevance Score, CPC is not a static number and should be checked daily. It is very common for your CPC to increase over time as your Relevance Score decreases due to stale ads and your targeted audience becomes saturated. Even the best ads which are considered evergreen ads because they can run months without being touched, will see a fluctuation in CPC.

I like looking at the Results, Reach and Impressions columns as well to get a percentage of people who have been exposed to the Ad compared to the potential total targeted audience and the percentage of people clicking on the Ad or Click Through Rate, CTR. In Module 2 you set your targeted audience and Facebook displayed the total potential amount of people that your Ad would be distributed to. If your Reach number is approaching the total potential audience then you know that your Ad is hitting its saturation point and your CPC is going to go up. The more important number to look at here though is CTR. Take the Result number and divide it by the Impressions number to get your CTR. Just with CPC, this number is going to fluctuate and more importantly the average CTR will vary by industry. The same website I mentioned in CPC will cover CTR by industry.

If you click on the Reports box towards the right of the screen a dropdown will appear showing different options. You can export the table data, create custom reports or share link along with a list of standard reports. I personally like to create my own reports that include other data for the Campaign not included with the Facebook Ads Manager such as revenue. That way I and those I share with them get a better picture of what is happening instead of exporting the table data. You may find these useful, so check them out to see for yourself how they may fit into your reporting needs.

You will want to check your Relevance Score on the Ads screen but your CPC and CTR should be check on the Campaign, Ad Sets and Ads pages. There may be more than one Ad per Ad Set and more than one Ad Set per Campaign as you get more comfortable with what Facebook advertising has to offer, you need to get into the habit of checking the data on all 3 screens. There is a plethora of reports that you can view and create within the Facebook Ads Manager but the above ones will be a good start to ensure you are monitoring your Ads properly. There are so many reports in fact that you could get lost in all the data and wasting your time doing that instead of doing things that will make you money. So just concentrate on the above data for now.

Module 4 Facebook Pixel & Basic Retargeting

The first three modules covered getting your Facebook business page setup, creating your first Facebook Ad and understanding the basics of Facebook data and reports generated from your ads. You are now up and running with people clicking on your ad, hitting your landing page and producing sales. But, how do you make sure you don't display the same ads to people who did or didn't convert on your landing page. The person who bought from you isn't going to want to continue to see your ads and it is a waste of your advertising budget to continue to do so. And if someone went to your landing page and didn't purchase, showing them the same ad isn't necessarily going to get them to change their mind. That is when you need the ability to retarget those who saw your first ad with subsequent ads that will cause a different reaction or purchase something else from you. Facebook gives you the tools to accomplish this, which begins with a small simple thing called the Facebook Pixel. Ever wonder how after you visit a website, you mysteriously see an ad on Facebook for the same thing, it is because that website is using the Facebook Pixel.

The Facebook Pixel is a small bit of code that is placed within your website code which you or your webmaster can perform. Each Facebook Ad account receives 1 Facebook Pixel. Simplistically the code tracks when someone arrives on your landing page from your Facebook ad. Like everything else in the first modules, you can do this as simply as you want or you really get intricate with the different types of Facebook Pixels that you place on the different pages of your website. I will start with the basic Pixel first and discuss the setup and functionalities of it and then I will give examples of how to utilize the advanced features.

To find your Facebook Pixel, go to your Ads Manager screen and click on the hamburger menu icon in between the Facebook icon and the words Ads Manager then click on All Tools in the popup menu. The box will expand and under the Measure & Report column, click on Pixels.

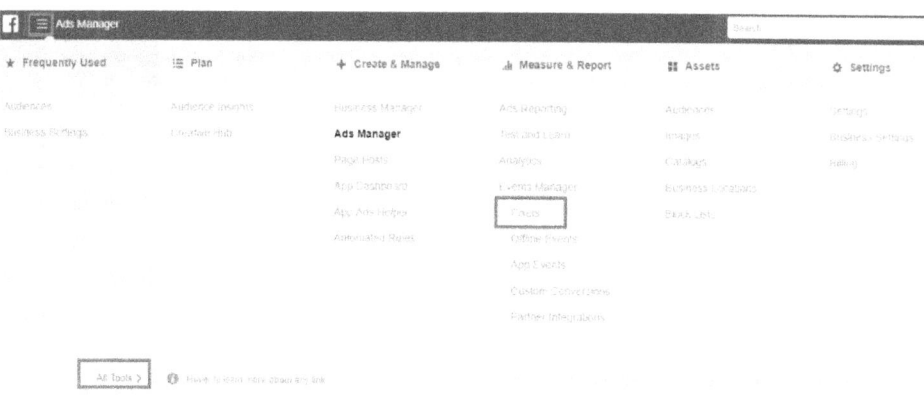

Since this is your first pixel, click on the green button that say Set Up Pixel.

You have three methods you can use to setup your pixel.

1. Use an Integration or Tag Manager. If you are using supported platforms such as Magento, Shopify, Big Commerce, WIX or others, you can integrate the Facebook Pixel without having to manually updating your website code. Just click on the icon to see if your platform is listed and to walk through the steps required to integrate your Facebook Pixel with your platform. Each platform listed will require a different setup procedure.
2. Manually Install the Code Yourself. This option or number 3 will be the most common methods that most people install their Facebook Pixel. If you are not comfortable adding a snippet of code to your website then I would suggest you let your website developer do so. Adding the basic Facebook Pixel code though is pretty easy and straight forward. Click on the icon and a box will open with 4 steps to follow.
    a. Step 1 tells you where to place the Facebook Pixel code and where to find the head tags in your code if you don't know where they are or what they look like.
    b. Step 2 displays your Facebook Pixel code for you to copy and paste into your website code.
    c. Step 3 gives you the option to turn on Automatic Advanced Matching. Anytime you can harness Facebook's power to track data and retarget your customers, you should take advantage of it, so turn it on.

d. Step 4 test to ensure your Facebook Pixel is installed properly and sending traffic to Facebook for tracking purposes.

Click on Next and head to the second part of setting up your Facebook Pixel which includes 3 more steps.

a. Step 1 is an informative area that explains how Facebook tracks events. You should spend time and read each section. This area will give you a better idea how to use the Facebook Pixel for more advanced tracking which requires adding code to various pages to track events such as when someone purchases, completes a registration, adds something to your cart and more.

b. Step 2 is where you turn on the different events that you want Facebook to track. For instance if you want to track when a person actually purchases, you would turn on the Purchase option and instructions open up with parameters you can set, the actual code to copy and paste, where to install the code and the ability to test the code. By creating the different event codes beyond the basic Facebook Pixel code installed earlier, you collect more data which helps you with your retargeting campaigns which will be discussed later in this module.

c. Step 3 allows you to install a Google Chrome extension called the Pixel Helper. If you are using Google Chrome, I strongly recommend you install this Chrome Extension. The purpose of the Pixel Helper is to allow you to see quickly if your Pixels are firing correctly on each individual page of your website.

After you have completed these steps by manually installing your Facebook Pixel, click on done.

3. Email instructions to a Developer. If you don't feel comfortable performing the steps by manually installing your Pixels then click on this icon. Fill in the e-mail address of your website developer, scroll down to the bottom of the block and click send. Your developer will receive the instructions on how to install your Facebook Pixel and they should be able to complete the task very quickly. I would recommend having a discussion with your developer concerning individual Event Codes to ensure the ones you want to utilize are installed and with the proper parameters. You should still install the Pixel Helper Chrome Extension though if you are using Google Chrome as your web browser so that you can monitor the status of your Facebook Pixels.

After your Facebook Pixel is installed and people are visiting your website pages, if you go back to the Pixel option in the menu shown above, Facebook will display statistics for your Pixel. Just like any of the other Facebook reports, you can choose options on what you want to see in the report. The report can be viewed with up to a maximum 30 days of data or you can just look at what is going on today. Data Sources include the Facebook Pixel, Offline Event Sets or App Events. If you create Apps then you can setup, measure and manage the actions on your app and use this data to find more customers. Offline Events measure how your Facebook Ads are affecting things such as your in-store sales if you have a physical store as well. And, with the more data Facebook gathers or is fed, the better it is able to assist you in making more sales by targeting your customers properly.

Now that you have your Facebook Pixel installed and it is collecting data, what do you do with it? The Facebook Pixel becomes your secret weapon of distributing ads that are pertinent for each customer at the stage of the buying process they are in. As you become more comfortable with Facebook marketing, you will want to have ads that are segmented towards particular customers. I am sure you have heard of or seen a picture of a marketing funnel. Just like a physical funnel is wide at the top to handle a large influx of whatever is being poured into it and it becomes smaller at the bottom which concentrates what is coming out of it. The marketing funnel performs the same way where lots of people who are clicking on your ads are pouring in but by the time they come out the other end only the most highly qualified customers who purchase will be pouring out. This training isn't going to get into all the intricacies of the marketing funnel but having a general idea of how it works will help utilize your Facebook Pixel to its fullest capabilities.

The Facebook Pixel is installed on the pages of your website gathering data about who is visiting. You can not see this data but Facebook is collecting personal information about each individual so that it can help create better targeted audiences for your Facebook ads. Let's take a look at a simple Facebook marketing strategy and how the Facebook Pixel will assist in making it successful.

You create your first Facebook Ad and hundreds a day or more are clicking on it and landing on your landing page. After looking at your data and reports, you realize that your CTR and CPC is and purchases are happening on your landing page. So, what do you do next?

For simplicity sake, you want to continue with your current ad for those who haven't been exposed to it yet. But, you need to retarget previous landing page viewers who didn't purchase with a different ad because you know that sometimes it takes 7 touches/views before most people convert. You also don't want these people to see your first ad. That is where the Facebook Pixel comes in.

And for those who did purchase, you will want to retarget that group with a different ad for an upsell and maintain a relationship with them so they purchase other products or services you offer.

A new Ad Set will need to be created and probably under the same Campaign. This is your choice, you can start a new Campaign or place it under the current Campaign, ensuring you name the Ad Set in a way that you can quickly tell the different Ad Sets apart and what each Ad Set's purpose is. Under Custom

Audiences on the Ad Set screen is the option to EXCLUDE people who are in at least ONE of the following: Custom Audience or Lookalike Audiences. (Custom Audiences and Lookalike Audiences is covered in Module 5. Facebook Pixel has to be installed and functioning before creating these audiences). Choose the appropriate audience which will be covered in Module 5 and now the new Ad you create under this Ad Set will not be displayed to those who saw the ad in #1.

I know this all very simplified but after you get your Facebook Pixel running and learn how to create Custom Audiences, in the next Module, from your website traffic of people who performed certain actions, you will be able to target and retarget your marketing in as many ways or as complicated as you want.

Module 5 Custom Audiences

The true excitement of Facebook advertising is the ability to harness Facebook's power and using it to your advantage. While everyone is spending hours on Facebook checking on what is going on with their friends, Facebook is also checking in on them. They are constantly gathering every piece of data that they can on every member of Facebook including e-mail address, phone numbers, likes, dislikes, friends, relatives and more. With 2.23 Billion active users that is a lot of data Facebook is storing which can be used to target your ideal audience with your ads. In an earlier module you learned how to use the preset audiences Facebook has created for everyone's basic uses. These audiences, although important to your marketing strategy, are cold leads which take more work to convert to sales and thus cost more to acquire. But what if by using the tools supplied by Facebook, you could rapidly target warm and even hot leads that will convert at a higher rate and cost less overall. The first step was to install the Facebook Pixel so that Facebook can start collecting data that you can use for marketing. In this module I will cover how to create different types of audiences from this data and from data you already possess in your customer databases.

First open the Ads Manager menu by clicking on the hamburger menu between the Facebook icon and Ads Manager and under Assets click on Audiences.

If this is your first audience, the following screen will open up with the options to create Custom Audience, Lookalike Audiences or Saved Audiences.

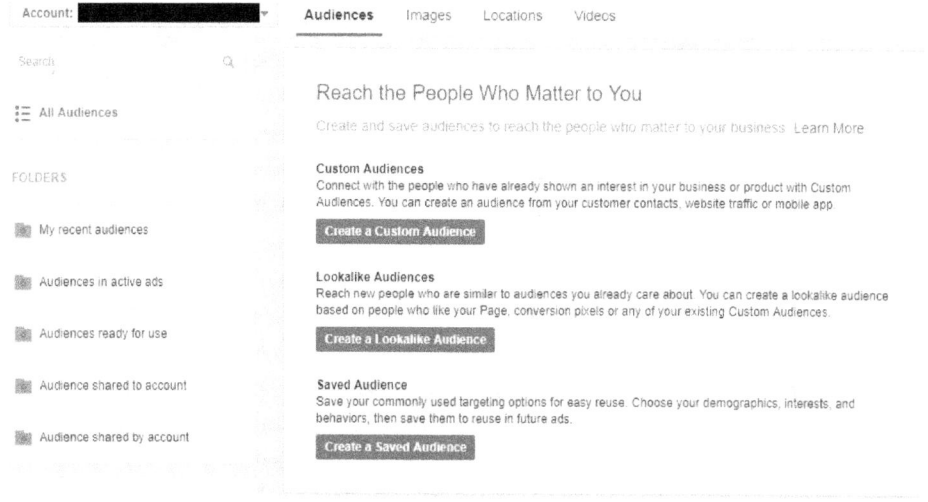

If you have already created your first audience, you will see a screen with those audiences listed and the button in the top left that says Create Audience which has a drop down to create Custom Audience, Lookalike Audience or Saved Audience.

Let's start by creating a Custom Audience. When you click on create a Custom Audience the following screen opens up displaying 5 different types of Custom Audiences that you can create. All 5 are important audiences to utilize in your Facebook marketing but I'm only going to go through how to create 2 of them in this module. If you understand how to create 1, you will understand how easy it is to just following Facebook's step by step process for each.

Create a Custom Audience

How do you want to create this audience?

Reach people who have a relationship with your business, whether they are existing customers or people who have interacted with your business on Facebook or other platforms.

Customer File
Use a customer file to match your customers with people on Facebook and create an audience from the matches. The data will be hashed prior to upload.

Website Traffic
Create a list of people who visited your website or took specific actions using Facebook Pixel.

App Activity
Create a list of people who launched your app or game, or took specific actions.

Offline Activity [UPDATED]
Create a list of people who interacted with your business in-store, by phone, or through other offline channels.

Engagement [UPDATED]
Create a list of people who engaged with your content on Facebook or Instagram.

This process is secure and the details about your customers will be kept private.

Cancel

The first Custom Audience we are going to create is the Customer File. This Custom Audience is created by using your current customer database. Facebook will take the file you are about to upload with your current customer information and go out and find those customer's profiles on Facebook. After Facebook finds your current customers, you will be able to target them with ads that are specific to them. The power of Facebook makes it easy to target your hottest customers, who have already done business with you. With the Custom Audience, you will also be able to find other Facebook users who have similar tastes as your current customers which I will cover later in creating Lookalike Audiences. So, let's click on Customer File and create our first Custom Audience.

Create a Custom Audience

Customer file

Add customers from your own file or copy and paste data
Use your customers' information to match them with people on Facebook.

Import from MailChimp
Import email addresses directly from this third-party connection by providing your login credentials.

Customer file with lifetime value (LTV)

Include LTV for better performing lookalikes [NEW]
Use a file with LTV to create a lookalike more similar to your most valuable customers.

Back

Most people will use the first option of Add customers from your own file or copy and paste data. Even if you have MailChimp, I wouldn't use this option unless your email list contains all the options that Facebook allows for uploading and you have the list segmented. Let's continue by clicking on Add customers from your own file or copy and paste data and clicking I Accept on the next screen concerning Things to Know About Custom Audiences.

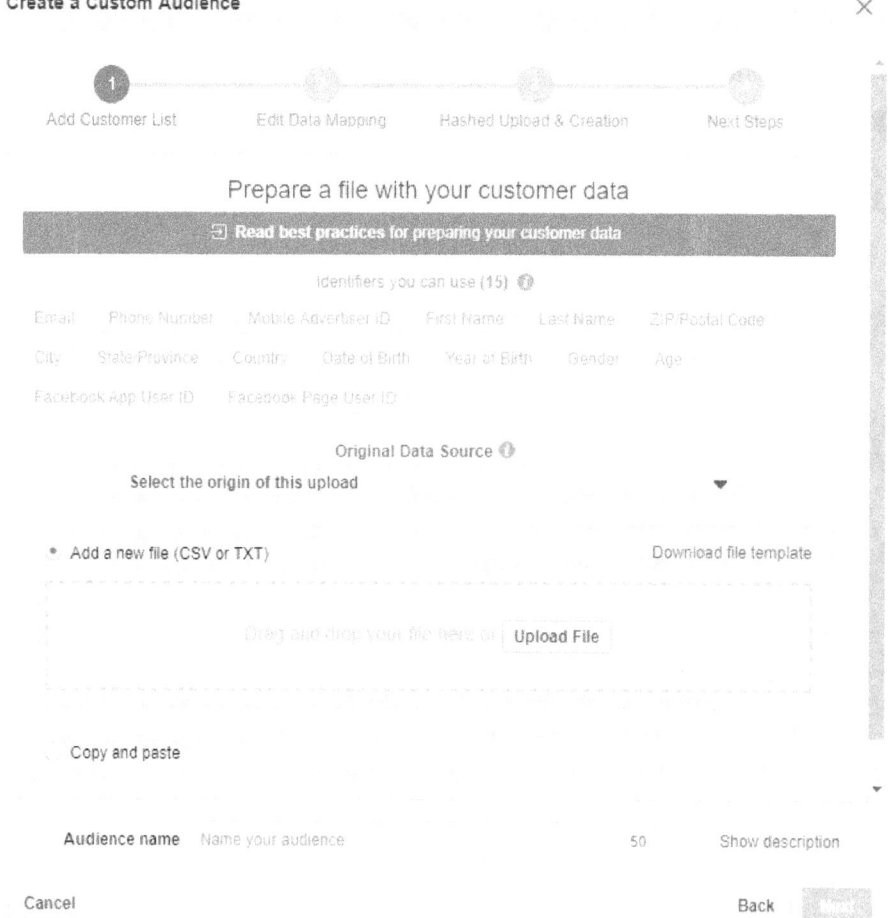

It is a step by step process now of uploading your customer data file.

1. Facebook has 15 identifiers that you can use in customer data file to help Facebook locate as many of your current customers as possible. If all you have is their first and last name, Facebook will not be able to segment your customer from everybody else when there are multiple people with the same name, so the more data you can feed Facebook, the better the list Facebook can compile for you.
2. The next item is where did you get your customer data. The best data is always sourced directly from your customers because you know the accuracy of it. So, select on the Origin of this upload, where you sourced the data from.
3. Next click on Upload File and locate it on your computer. The file has to be a CSV or TXT file. If you are uncertain as to what the file should look like, Facebook has the option to download a file template.
4. Give your audience name in the Audience Name line. Be as descriptive as possible so that you know who is in this particular audience, when the audience was created and so forth. Click next when ready.

5. You are now given the option to preview and map your identifiers. Sometimes Facebook won't recognize what a column is or there may be columns included in your data which aren't apart of the 15 Facebook identifiers in step 1. After you are satisfied with the mapping then click on Upload & Create.

6. A screen will appear showing that the file is being uploaded to Facebook. After the upload completes you will be taken back to the main Audience screen where your now created audience will be displayed, with the name, type of audience it is, size, availability and date created. At first the screen will show that your audience is updating, which means Facebook is going through all of their records and locating your customers. The time it takes depends on the size of the list you uploaded. After Facebook has completed their search, availability will state Ready with a green dot. You can also compare the total number of customers that you uploaded versus what Facebook was able to locate in the size column.

Your first custom audience is now ready to be used when you pick audiences during the Ad Set process or create Lookalike Audiences. Before we create a Lookalike Audience, let's create another Custom Audience. This time choose Website Traffic and the following screen appears.

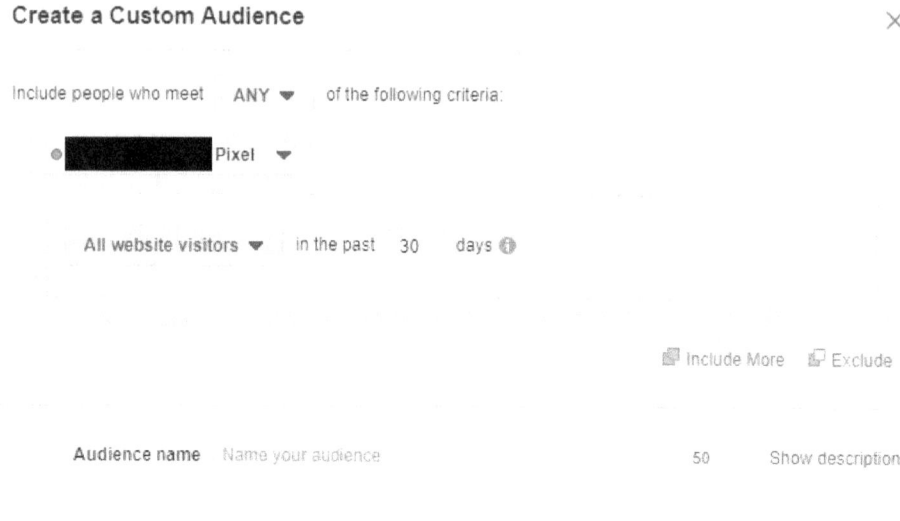

1. Line one pick if people meet either ANY or ALL of the following criteria. If you choose ALL then the person has to meet every criteria listed but if you pick ANY then the person only has to meet 1 of the criteria listed.
2. The next line should display the Facebook Pixel name you created in module 4 and is currently running on your landing page.
3. Next you will choose to have all website visitors collected or if you click on the dropdown arrow you can choose other options for collection. If you choose another option besides all website visitors then you will have to input other data to assist Facebook with who to collect. Progressing along that line choose how many days in the past you want collected with a maximum of 180 days. This is useful when you want to create Custom Audiences for retargeting ads to

ensure people are getting fresh content along the funnel process.
4. The ability to make this is as simple or complex that you want to make it. Facebook gives you the ability to include more people into this audience or even exclude people. Excluding people would be used to exclude someone who purchased a product and you don't want to display a retargeting ad to them encouraging them to purchase what they already purchased.
5. Give your audience name in the Audience Name line. Be as descriptive as possible so that you know who is in this particular audience, when the audience was created and so forth. Then click Create Audience.

After you click Create Audience, you will receive a screen stating that your Custom Audience was created and the option to perform two more steps of finding new people similar to your existing users or Lookalike Audience and create an ad using the audience. I am going to discuss creating Lookalike Audiences next so just click Done. Your new Custom Audience will now appear above your previous Custom Audience. Feel free to experiment with the other 3 Custom Audience options and find the Custom Audience that works best for your marketing needs. The more you harness the power of Facebook, the better your ads will perform.

Let's create a Lookalike Audience now. When you create a Lookalike Audience, you are telling Facebook to take your Custom Audience and go out and find like minded people in the vastness of Facebook users. As everyone knows,

Facebook collects a ton of information on its' users and this is your opportunity to take advantage of that to find new customers that may like your product as much as your current customers.

Create a Lookalike Audience

Find new people on Facebook who are similar to your existing audiences. Learn more

Source — Choose a Custom Audience or a Page
Create new ▼

Location — Search for countries or regions to target   Browse

Audience Size

0 1 2 3 4 5 6 7 8 9 10 % of countries

Audience size ranges from 1% to 10% of the total population in the countries you choose, with 1% being those who most closely match your source.

Show Advanced Options ▼

Cancel   Create Audience

1. Click on the Source line and pick the Custom Audience that you want to find similar people on Facebook. Your Custom Audience needs to have at least 100 people in it for Facebook to create a Lookalike Audience.
2. Pick United States for Location unless you are advertising in other countries.
3. For Audience Size you can pick between 1% to 10% of that county's total population on Facebook that is similar to your Custom Audience. The temptation will be to choose 10% to achieve a larger audience size but

the further you get away from 1% the less similar someone will be. It is recommended to stick around 1 - 3% to achieve the best Lookalike Audience size.
4. If you click on Advanced Options, the process will create 3 different audience sizes for you and display what the audience size will be for those. You may want to try this a few times to assist you in determining which Lookalike size produces the best for you.

Due to the size of a Lookalike Audience and the amount of data Facebook sorts through, it takes a while before it is Ready for you to use.

Custom Audiences and Lookalike Audiences have an almost unlimited possibility of combinations that you can work with. The smaller the audience and more specific the segment, the better for targeting and testing what ads work the best for your product. Your cost overall will also diminish as you dial in your targeting and ad creation.

Now that you have these Custom and Lookalike Audiences, where do you utilize them in your ad creation. In module 2 we discussed the steps under the Audience section of Ad Sets and we bypassed the section that says Custom Audiences. Now you can pick your Custom Audience or Lookalike Audience to use in this section. You can still pick a specific location if you are targeting a local area but you don't need to pick any of the options in detailed targeting. When you use the option of utilizing Custom Audiences there is also an option to exclude a particular Custom Audience. This is helpful if you have created a Custom Audience of those who purchased a particular product from you but you don't want these people to see the same top of the funnel ad for that product again.

Now take the your Custom Audiences and combine them with the Facebook Pixel and you can truly retarget select groups with the best ad to get new cold leads, massage warm leads or close the deal with hot leads. More on the Facebook Sales Funnel will be covered in Module 9.

It seems like I keep repeating myself but you can get as simple or as complex with this as you see fit for your Facebook marketing. There is no reason not to take advantage of the power of Facebook, they give you the tools and want to see you succeed.

Module 6 A/B Testing & Defining Audiences

At this point you should have a good grasp of the fundamentals of Facebook marketing and how to create ads, custom audiences and analyzing the results of your ads. Finding the perfect ad on the first attempt most likely won't happen unless you have been doing Facebook Ads for awhile and even then the experienced person won't hit a homerun every time. There are so many variables that can and will impact your ads such as what works in one city, doesn't work another city. The demographics of the United States across all 50 states is diverse and then if you start advertising outside of the US things can change even more dramatically. So, what is the best way to find the best ad for your product and produces the results you are expecting and looking for? Testing different ads with different variables is the answer. The term used most often is A/B testing because you run 2 different ads at the same time to determine which is the most effective. With Facebook marketing though you will often find yourself running more than 2 ad variations at a time to determine the best ad to run for your campaign.

I covered the basics of creating a Campaign with one Ad Set and one Ad in the previous modules and briefly mentioned the ability to create multiple Ad Sets under a Campaign and multiple Ads under an Ad Set. This is where you will find the ability to test different ads and compare them efficiently. Let's take a visual look at the possibilities.

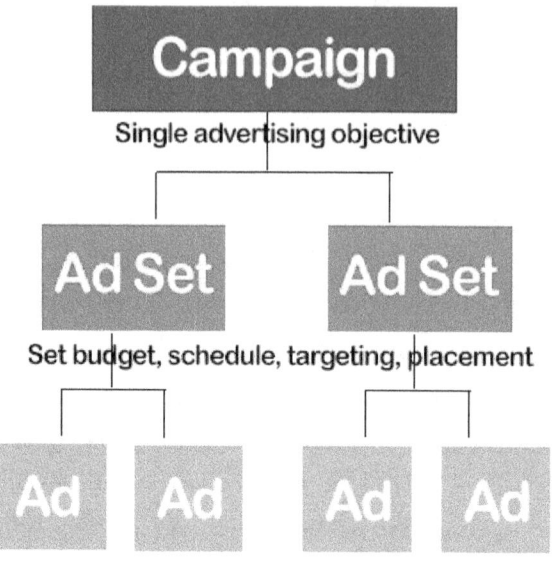

The above diagram only shows 2 Ad Sets under Campaign but you can create as many as you want and the same is true for Ads under Ad Set. I have seen diagrams that had 10 Ad Sets and 10 Ads under each Ad Set totally 100 different Ads running for one Campaign. Just as I have mentioned in previous modules, you can make this as simple or as complex as you want or need. Let's break down the above diagram.

1. Campaign – The Campaign is a single advertising objective such as driving traffic to your landing page or post engagements on your page. It is the top tier level of your Facebook advertising. Remember to name your Campaign in a way that describes what your objective is and that just about anyone who sees it, understands what the result of the campaign should be.

2. Ad Set – This will be the first level where you can A/B test your Facebook advertising or run different variables for your funnel or other needs. Remember in the Ad Set you can set the targeting of who sees your Ad and where they see it. If this is a brand new Ad Set, you essentially will be guessing what to set but you should know your audience well enough to at least make an educated guess. So, if you are A/B testing you could set one Ad Set to target those in your Customer Audience which includes your customers, set one Ad Set to target those in a Lookalike Audience and set another that includes those who have a specific interest. Another example utilizing the idea of a funnel would be set one Ad Set to target cold customers who are seeing your ad for the first time and excludes visitors to your landing page, one set to include a Custom Audience of those who visited your landing page and another set to include a Custom Audience of those who purchased from your landing page. Besides testing target audiences you could also test the placement of your ads to see if they work better on mobile, desktop or the other placement options. Any of the options that can be configured under the Ad Set ultimately can be used for creating multiple Ad Sets under a Campaign. Note: Remember the Ad Set tier is where you dictate how much money is spent so all Ads created under an Ad Set share the that particular Ad Set's budget.
3. Ad – At the Ad tier level, you can create as many Ads as you want under a particular Ad Set. All the Ads under an Ad Set share the same budget, targeting and placements that were set in the Ad Set they fall under. You can create

Ads with different images, text, call-to-actions (CTA), or links. This proves very useful in finding the right combination of images and text that people respond well to and ultimately click on your link to your landing page. After you have determined the best image and text combination and you see great results of people clicking to your landing pages, you may still may not be seeing the results you would expect. You may find out it is your landing page not your ad that needs tweaking. So, if you have the resources to create multiple style landing pages, you can test different links in Ads to determine which of your landing pages produces the best as well.

Take the time and diagram out your Ad Sets and Ads on a sheet of paper or better yet create a spreadsheet. On the spreadsheet, create a column for all of the information for each variable and create additional columns for data from the reports. A spreadsheet will enable you to quickly see which Ad Sets and Ads are performing the best for engagement and cost.

So, how long should you run an ad to determine if it is actually performing to your expectations? When you first launch your Ad Set, Facebook starts what they call a learning phase. During the learning phase, Facebook is determining what it will take to run your Ad Set the most effective way for you to get the best results. Facebook states the learning phase takes at least 50 stabilized events to achieve stable delivery of your ad. If you make any significant changes to your Ad Set or Ad, the learning phase will restart. Stopping an Ad Set or Ad before the learning phase is over and before Facebook can utilize its' algorithms will not give you a true indication whether it was performing well or not. The answer to how long you should run an Ad Set or Ad to determine if it is performing to your expectation is typically 7 days. I have found though that typically I will recognize if I should edit or shut down an Ad Set or Ad in 4 days. Unless you are using a previous Ad Set that is proven, start your new Ad Sets with a lower dollar budget for testing. After you have experienced 4 – 7 days of achieving your expectations from the Ad Set, then increase your budget in order to ramp up your results.

There are Ad Sets that seem to be able to handle as high a budget as can be thrown at them and perform with high results of people clicking to landing pages and maintaining a low cost of running. But, at the same time there are plenty more Ad Sets that have what I call the point of diminishing return. These Ad Sets increase in cost of obtaining a new customer as time progressives and throwing more money at the Ad Set doesn't improve things but actually increases the cost sometimes. This is why it is important to check your Facebook reports daily. Remember in the Ad Set you set the target audience and that audience only has so many potential people associated with it. The higher the budget allocated, the more potential people will have your ad displayed in their feed. After you find that perfect Ad Set and Ad, you may allocate $100 per day to display your ad to an estimated 15000 people a day out of a potential 150,000 and find the Cost Per Click to be 44 cents. A week later that good ad may now be costing 88 cents a day and you have already exposed your ad to 105,000 people. Increasing your budget isn't going to decrease the cost of your ad because you only have about 45,000 people left in your targeted audience and Facebook hasn't exposed them yet because they know those people of the least likely to respond to an offer in an ad. So every Ad Set will have a targeted audience (even those targeting a whole country will run out of people to display a particular ad) that will have a point where it is no longer cost effective to increase the spend but lower it may still be effective.

This all seems like a lot of work but when you get everything dialed in and find that right combination of Ad Sets and Ads, things will get easier. The key is to not get discouraged at the beginning when you aren't getting the exact results you were expecting. Facebook advertising requires time and patience and the fact you don't have to spend a lot to create your ad, you can afford to spend the time needed to test and re-test until you get it right. Too often those who state that Facebook advertising doesn't work, didn't spend the time necessary to test their ads and use Facebook's tools to analyze the reports in order to find the ad that works best for their product. Just remember to track your results and monitor the reports daily to ensure you know when the best time will be to edit an ad, adjust the budget or halt it altogether.

Part of your testing and using different Ad Sets is the ability to target the correct audience and targeting the best size of audience. We covered creating Custom and Lookalike Audiences in the previous module but when creating the best Ad Sets as discussed in this module, you need to narrow it down even more to get the best results. Let's take your Custom Audience of your current customer database. The customer database may consist of 1,000,000 people who have interacted with you through your website, e-mails, store visits, contests, etc.. But did every one of those 1,000,000 purchase your product, how many have actually read your emails and how many have only had a passing interaction with you. You will not want to have the different groups of people in your database be displayed the same ad on their Facebook feed because each group needs to be treated differently in order to get them to purchase your product. This is where segmenting your audiences into smaller groups increases the effectiveness of your Facebook advertising and lower the costs.

Segmenting your audiences will be very useful in the next Module 9 which discusses integrating Facebook advertising and funnels. Examples of segmented audiences would be: hot leads or those who have already purchased from you, cold leads or those who have never interacted with you, warm leads or those who have interacted but never purchased anything from you, website visitors, those who have engaged with your Facebook posts or any other category that suites your marketing needs.

So, what is that number you should be shooting for in an audience size? It is the sweet spot between ensuring it is specific enough to get results from that segment of people and large enough for Facebook to use its' power to optimize your ads for best results. In most circumstances that number will be between 500,000 – 1,000,000. More than 1 million and you run the risk that Facebook won't find enough people that would be interested in your ad and start showing it to people who don't typically click on promotions or ads. Less than 500,000 and Facebook may not have enough results to optimize your ad. There are going to be instances where you won't have enough people to reach 500,000 for instance if you are a local business and where you live doesn't have that much population.

It is easier to sell hot and warm leads or customers and the cost will be less expensive and it will be hard to sell cold leads and the cost will increase to convert them into paying customers. It is always best to go after the low lying fruit first and then concentrate on the others which will take more effort of testing and adjusting your ads. Just keep in mind that the more you segment your audience the better you will be able to analyze which ads produce the most conversions, are the most cost effective and ultimately put the most money in your pocket. And as I have mentioned multiple times, Facebook gives you so many tools here that you can make this as simple or as complex as you want.

Module 7 Facebook Ad Formats

Through all the previous modules, I've only addressed creating Ads that comprised of 1 static image but there are other options available in Facebook. The single static image is functional but the other options have better results and a couple are even more cost effective. Using one of the other options may require more effort in setting up but in the long run they will prove more beneficial to achieve your ultimate results. Video ads typically have high relevancy scores and the CPC is typically much lower than single image ads.

The options available are listed in the Ad section in the Format box and include Carousel, Single Image (already covered in Module 2), Single Video, Slideshow and Collection. I will go through each one by one and explain how to utilize it and the benefits of each.

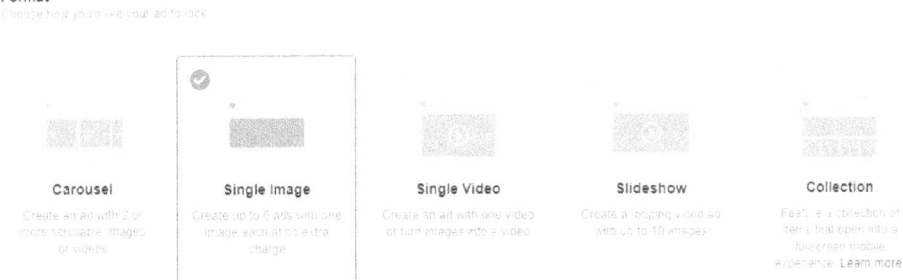

1. Carousel – The Carousel format allows you to use 2 or more images or videos that are scrollable when the ad is displayed in someone's Facebook feed. There are different ways you can use the Carousel including; displaying different products that are offered, show a sequence of

events or different view points of a single product. The process of setting up a Carousel with multiple images/videos has a few extra steps compared to a single image which was covered in module 2.

    a. Click on Carousel and current options rearrange and other options appear than with a single image. You will notice from the Mobile Feed view that there a multiple images or as Facebook refers to them cards in the preview pane and as you scroll down the options these cards scroll with you.

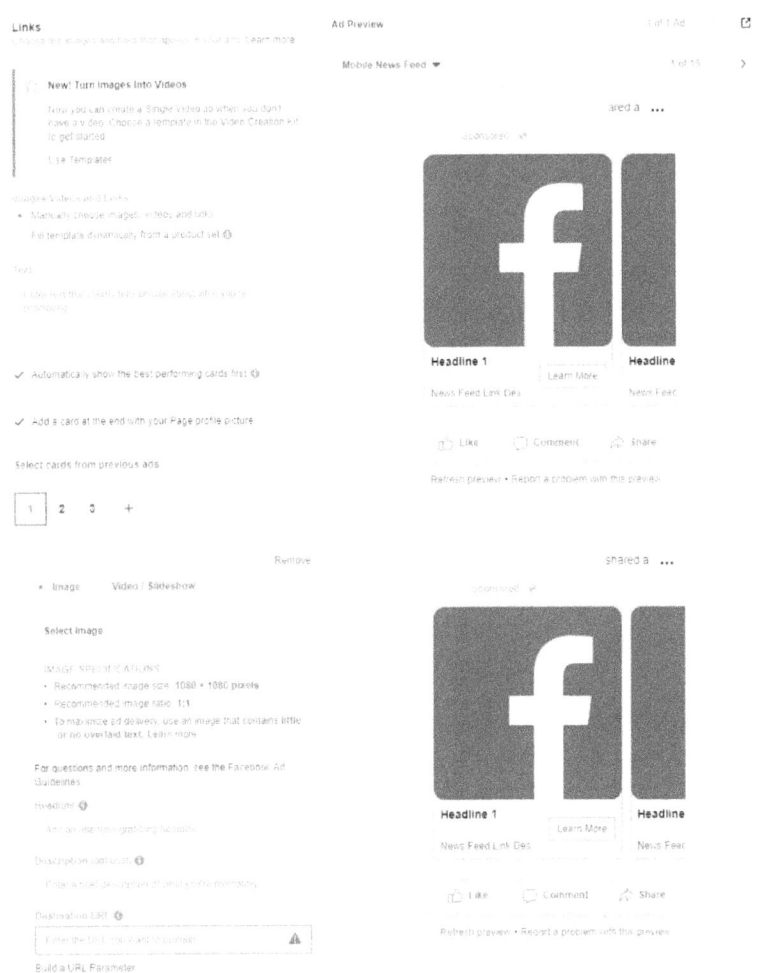

b. The first thing this time is to fill in the text for the ad. The text you enter here will appear above all of the cards.

c. Moving down there is a check mark by default in the box next to Automatically show the best performing cards first. Most often you will leave this default because you want the best performing picture first

so that you get the most results. You would uncheck this box if for example your pictures tell a story in sequence such as making a cake and the News Feed Description correlates with the sequence.
d. Next by default a box is checked by Add a card at the end with your Page profile picture. There may be times you find this useful but for the most part your Page profile picture isn't going to create you more conversions. I would uncheck that box unless you are creating a campaign promoting your company specifically.
e. The next step is where you will determine how many cards will compose your carousel. The minimum is 2 and the maximum is 10 for a carousel. It is recommended to remain between 3 – 5 cards due to the attention span of most people, they won't view anything past 5 cards unless it is a compelling ad that tells a story. To add more cards just click on the plus sign and remove a card just highlight the number and click on remove. Ensure number 1 is highlighted for the first card to prepare for the next step.
f. I'm going to just deal with static images here for the cards because it is simpler and I can't screen capture a video to display my examples. But there are many great examples on the web of how companies have utilized the carousel to tell a story with video for their ads. Before you pick your image to populate your first card, you need to ensure it meets the

recommended image size of 1080x1080 pixels. Ensure you don't use the same picture you utilized for a single image ad which is 1200x628 pixels. After you have your image ready click on Select Image and add it to the first card.

g. The Headline is similar to adding a Headline single image ad except the Headline this time is only for this card. You can have a different headline for each card in your Carousel. You can get as creative as you want here particularly if you are telling a story or a sequence like making a cake.

h. The same thing goes for the Description section. The Description is specific for this card only and you can have a different description for each card. So here is what card 1 looks like.

Time to create your next card by click on number 2 above where you select the image. To see the preview of what you are creating, click on the right arrow in the preview pane. Now repeat steps f thru h from above. And repeat this for the number of cards you want in your carousel. Below is an example of a 3 card carousel with the second card centered.

Sponsored

Are in need of a vacation? Would it feel good to disconnect for awhile?

You can at this remote gem. Sleep in luxurious bungelows surrounded by crystal blue water and private beaches. Leave the stress of work behind and re-energize your mind and body.

Learn More

Walk hand in hand along a secluded beach
Reserve your dream vacation now!

Learn More

Explore the Spl World
Welcome to Par

After you have completed creating your cards and you are satisfied with everything, scroll down and click Publish. It takes Facebook longer to approve Video ads so don't panic if a couple of hours go by before you receive the your ad is approved message.

2. Single Video – The Single Video is similar to Single Image but instead of using a static image, you will use a video. It is recommended that videos are less than 15 seconds but Facebook can display videos that are 240 minutes long. The diagram below shows all the video specifications needed to display in different locations. Essentially if you want your video to display across all the possible locations it needs to be no more than 15 seconds long. The steps to setup a Single Video ad are fairly simple. The creation of your video and making sure it is compelling to watch to the end will be your toughest task.

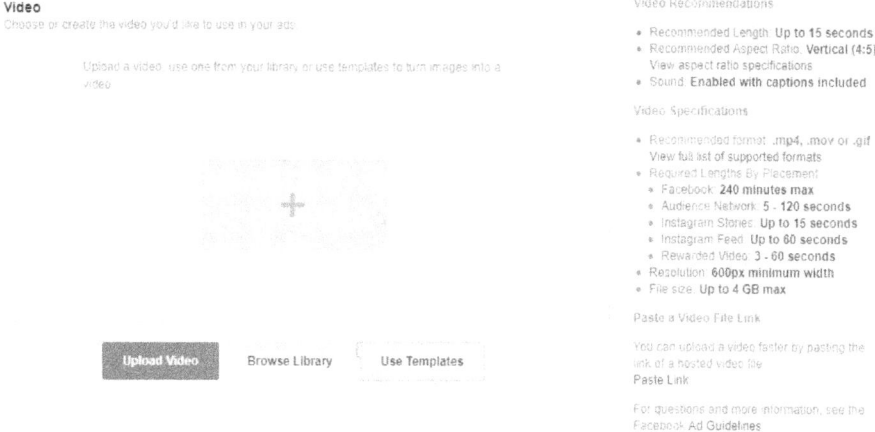

   a. Click on Single Video and the above screen will open up which looks very similar to a single image, only this time you are uploading a video or choosing one from your library. After your video loads in the preview screen move on to the next step.

b. The next steps are identical as setting up a Single Image ad. Fill in your Text, Website URL, Headline and News Feed Link Description and then click Publish.

3. Slideshow - The Slideshow is exactly what it sounds like. You are able to create a looping video with up to 10 image and you need a minimum of 3 images. Sort of sounds like the Carousel but the difference is that all images in the Slideshow have the same Text and Headline and they rotate automatically where the Carousel, the viewer has to advance the cards manually.

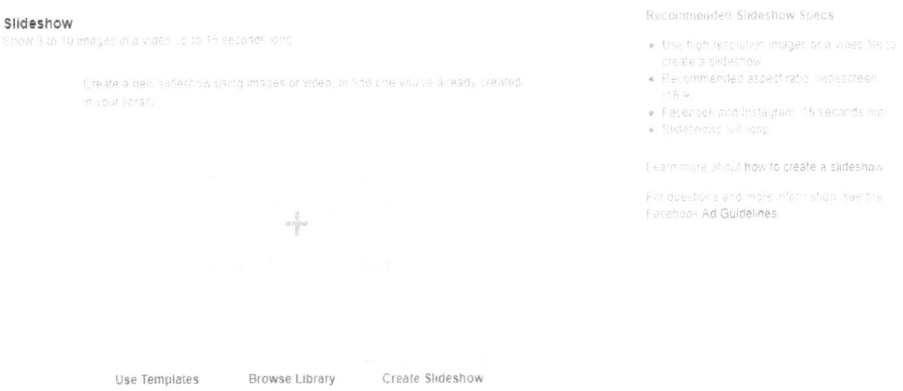

a. Click on Slideshow and above screen will open up.
b. Click on the + sign to add your images for the Slideshow and you get the following popup screen.

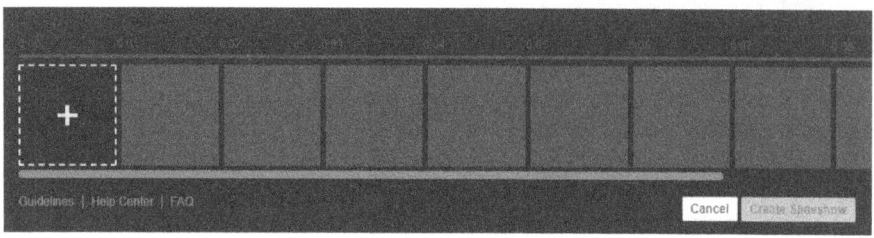

c. First you can choose the Aspect Ration of your images. The options are Square (1:1), Rectangle (16:9) or Vertical (2:3).
d. Next choose the Image Duration of your images between 0.5 and 5 seconds. Keep in mind that your Slideshow can not be longer than 15 seconds.
e. Next choose your Transition between the images, either None or Fade.
f. You have two ways to perform the next step of actually adding your images. Either click on Add Photos or the + sign in the Slideshow strip, they take you to the same location where you will choose or upload your images.
g. After you have chosen your images and they populate the Slideshow strip, just click on Create Slideshow.

h. The last steps are identical as Single Image and Single Video. Fill in your Text, Website URL, Headline and News Feed Link Description and then click Publish.

Note: The example shown created a Slideshow with static images. You can create a Slideshow as well with videos that you previously have created.

4. Collection – The Collection option is not a video but a collection of items that open up in a mobile screen and makes it easier to browse and purchase items directly from their mobile device. I am not going to cover this option but Facebook has provided templates and in depth information if you choose to explore making a Collection.

Video is proving to be the best form of advertising. People are more apt to view a video that gives them more information than viewing just a static image. You don't see images going viral but everyday there is a new viral video being uploaded and discovered. Video ads may take more work to setup because you have to create the video and make it compelling but the cost to run it is typically much cheaper and converts much better.

BONUS: I generically described how to create Video ads in Facebook but seeing examples of well done ads will help you visualize the possibilities.

Carousel: https://www.facebook.com/carouselformat A group that shares good examples of
Carousel ads

Single Video: A quick search for Best Facebook Video Ad Examples will supply you with days of video to watch.

Slideshow: https://www.facebook.com/slideshowads/ A group that shares good examples of Slideshow ads

Module 8 Facebook Marketing Objectives

Facebook Ads Manager offers many different Marketing Objectives to choose from depending on what you are trying to accomplish. Up to this point, I've only addressed the basic Traffic objective of getting as many people to click through your ad and arrive on your landing page. Facebook breaks the Marketing Objectives down into 3 categories of Awareness, Consideration and Conversion with each having multiple options to choose from. I am going to cover each option but will not get into all the differences that occur in the step by step process of creating the ad from start until you click on publish. By the time you are branching out and trying different objectives, you will have gotten a firm grasp of how Facebook steps through the set up procedures for Ad Sets and Ads.

The first Objective is Awareness with the options of Brand Awareness and Reach. The Objective of Awareness is to generate interest in your product, service or company. The goal is to reach as many people as possible to let them know about you and not to necessarily make a conversion

1. Brand Awareness objective is to do exactly that, increase awareness concerning your product, service or company. The goal is to get people to remember your product, service or company when a situation arises that they find a need for your item. Examples of this would be Apple, Microsoft, McDonald's, Walmart. All these companies are engrained in people's minds through brand awareness marketing. This objective is best suited for large businesses who have the budget to create awareness without the

concern to create an immediate conversion which increases the cost to run this particular type of ad. Facebook will default to delivering this objective through impressions since the goal is to create awareness by displaying your ad to as many people as possible. This leads to needing a higher budget because you will be charged every time Facebook displays your ad.
2. Reach objective is similar to Brand Awareness but this time Facebook will display your ad to the maximum amount people as possible. The difference is that when it comes to ad delivery you are able to set a frequency cap of how many impressions during a set number of days that someone will see your ad. This is helpful to prevent ad fatigue due to people getting tired of seeing your ad all of the time and thus creating a negative instead of a positive perception of your product, service or company.

The next Objective is Consideration with the options of Traffic, Engagement, App Installs, Video Views, Lead Generation, and Messages. This goal is to get people to consider your product, service or company and to be interested in clicking your ad to find out more information.

1. Traffic objective is useful in getting people clicking from your ad to your landing page to learn more about your product, service or company. It is the most generic objective available and most widely used one. It is the objective used for all examples in previous modules.
2. Engagement objective helps get more people to see and engage with a current post on your Page or your Page. You

would use this to increase comments, shares, likes, responses and claim offers. The Engagement objective will assist you in getting posts on your Page or any updates on your Page that you want your current audience to be aware of or help find new people who may be interested in your Page. For ad delivery options you will be able to choose Post Engagement by default, Impressions or Daily Unique Reach and will be charge by Impressions.
3. App Installs objective is exactly that, your ad will send people to an App Store to download your app. Set up options will allow you to pick which App Store your app is located and type in the name of your app. You will be able to choose Impressions or Link Clicks to be charged for this type of ad.
4. Video Views objective promotes videos that you want people to watch about your product, service or company. Facebook optimizes this ad to be placed in front of as many people as possible that typically watch videos in their News Feed. Options during setup of Video Views including Optimization for Ad Delivery of either   10 Second Video Views and 2 Second Video Views and when you get charged by either Impression or 10 Second Video View. Although, Impressions typically require a higher budget, when it comes to Video Views they are typically a lot less expensive. Videos have a 15 second maximum length when utilizing the Video View objective so be sure they are as compelling as possible for the time allotted.
5. Lead Generation objective assists in collecting lead information from people who want to learn more about

your product, service or company. When a person clicks on your Lead Generation ad a form automatically pops up pre-populated with the person's information that is stored in Facebook. All they have to do then is click on submit and you receive the lead. The downside to collecting leads this way instead of your own landing page are, people don't keep their email addresses up to date on Facebook so the email address could be wrong and you can't supply them with any other additional information about your product, service or company. You will be charged per impression for this type of ad.

6. Messages objective get more people to have conversations with your company through Messenger or WhatsApp for purchases, customer service or support. This objective will require more manpower and time if you utilize a live person to monitor and answer all the messages. There is an option to utilize bots to answer the messages but people typically can tell if a bot is responding and will be more likely to work with a company that offers the individual attention of a live person. You will be charged per impression for this type of ad.

The final objective is Conversion with the options of Conversions, Catalog Sales and Store Visits. This objective is to encourage people to move past information gathering and actually purchase your product or service.

1. Conversions objective is to get people from your Facebook ad to take action and move to your landing page where they will claim an offer or make an actual purchase. The Ad

Delivery options in setup are by default Conversions, Landing Page Views and Link Clicks. You can also adjust the conversion window: After Clicking Ad of 1 or 7 days or After Clicking Or Viewing Ad of 1 day click or view or 7 days click or 1 day view. You will be charged per impression for this type of ad unless you change the Ad Delivery to Link Clicks then you have the option to be charge by Impression or Link Click.

2. Catalog Sales objective creates ads that automatically show items from your catalog based on your target audience. Catalogs won't be covered in any of the modules but you can find Catalogs listed in the Ads Manager menu under Assets. After supplying a Campaign Name you will choose which Catalog you want to utilize before moving onto creating the Ad Set. A pixel must be assigned to your Catalog for any of the Ad Set options to function properly. The Ad Set has a section for choosing Product Sets to promote and different Audience options to select. You will be charged either by Link Click or Impression depending on which you choose for this ad type.

3. Store Visits allows you to promote multiple business locations to people near where they are located. After you supply a Campaign Name you will choose a Facebook Page. If you do not have your business locations already set up in Business Manager, you will be asked to do that prior to continuing. You can click on Learn More for directions on how to set up your multiple business locations. During set up of the objective you will have multiple options to configure depending on how many

locations you have and how you group them. With Store Visits you won't be able to track exactly your conversions but you will be able to see per location the ad traffic that is occurring and compare that to the increased foot traffic in your store. You could also place an offer on the ad and track how often it is used in your store.

There are 11 Marketing Objectives categorized in 3 areas of Awareness, Consideration and Conversion. You will most likely never use all 11 of the objectives but it is advisable to test and try a few of the objectives to see which one works best for your marketing. Most likely you will find 2 or 3 of the objectives will be required to meet all of your needs at some point as you grow your business.

Module 9 Facebook Sales Funnel

You have become an expert at creating Facebook Ads and they are your cheapest way of advertising but are they being the most effective for you for your marketing efforts. If you aren't using sales funnels then you probably are spending more than you need to in Facebook advertising, not reaching the complete audience possible and not getting the best conversions from ad to landing page and ultimately a sale. This is where you take everything you have learned about creating different types of audiences, data analysis, and retargeting and put it all together to achieve your most effective Facebook advertising.

There has been a lot of research and testing to determine the best sales funnel strategy which could occupy a month's time of you reading and in the end just being confused and frustrated. There are diagrams that show a sales funnel having 3 steps and some having upwards of 10 steps so my goal is to keep it as simple as possible. What it comes down to is your ability to understand the basics and adapt it to your particular marketing needs.

So, what is a sales funnel? Imagine a funnel you use in a kitchen with a wide opening at one end which is the entrance and a narrow opening at the other end or exit. For a sales funnel the wide opening is where hundreds of potential leads are entering everyday but you know not all of those people are going to take action on your offer. As you make offers down the funnel, only people that are truly interested will move down to those offers. And by the time you get to the end of the funnel which is where your main offer is, only people who are qualified leads will be left.

The following diagram demonstrates a basic sales funnel that you would utilize with Facebook advertising.

To begin your sales funnel, first you need to attract potential leads or create awareness of your product, service or company. These are cold leads, people who do not know anything about your product, service or company and don't know why they should be interested in you. There are more of them and they cost the most to obtain. The best way of doing this, is by creating posts on your Facebook page which are engaging and relevant and/or create Facebook ads that get people to engage with your Facebook page or landing page. Engagement includes commenting, liking or sharing your Facebook posts, liking your Facebook page, visiting your landing page, or collecting email addresses on your landing page. Module 4 discussed the importance of the Facebook Pixel and it is extremely important to have when working with a Facebook sales funnel. The Facebook Pixel will assist in tracking everyone who interacted with your landing page and Facebook will track everyone who engages with your Facebook posts and page.

The second step is to start retargeting everyone that has engaged with your Facebook page and landing page. These are now warm leads, they are beginning to understand why they would be interested in your product, service or company and require a more specific Facebook ad so that they want to move forward in a relationship with you. How to retarget audiences was covered in Module 4 but what do you retarget these potential leads with? The best thing to offer people are free or low cost items to fulfill such as eBooks, webinar, videos, discounts or even a phone call. Anything that the customer will see as a value to them for exchange of their time and information will work. You will lose some people as this process progresses but the ones that stay are truly interested in what you have to offer and the chances of a sale and a permanent customer increases. You may not need another step before the end of the funnel but in some cases you may need to add another retargeting stage where you are building more trust with the leads. You will need to experiment to find what works best for your marketing plan.

The final step in a funnel is making the main sale. Congratulations, the leads left at this point have demonstrated that they are interested in your product or service and want to purchase from you. These are hot leads who understand why they want to buy from you and are willing to enter into a long term relationship with you. Just because you have successfully moved people through your funnel, your work isn't done yet.

Now it is time to analyze the data and every aspect of your Facebook ads and your funnel. Is there something you can do better, a tweak here and tweak there? The goal is to get an evergreen Facebook sales funnel that doesn't need to be touched and will constantly feed your funnel. But, remember Facebook, demographics, people's wants and needs are always changing so analyzing your Facebook sales funnel often is needed, maybe not everyday but at least once a week.

This is just a basic concept for Facebook sale funnel and like everything else discussed in all of the Modules, you can make it as simple or as complex as you want. I wouldn't stop though when someone makes a purchase at the end of your funnel. Your hot leads will be your most profitable group to market to and the cost of Facebook ads to this group will be a lot less expensive. You now have a customer that has expressed interest in your company, how do you maintain them as a customer for life? Constant communication through newsletters, contests, promotions and updates will keep that new customer nurtured and feel a connection with your company. A nurtured customer will then be easy to upsell to a more advanced product or any other product you sell. A happy customer also has the potential to leave positive reviews and even refer friends and family who will help feed your funnel.

Every funnel will have a different success rate of what the percentage of people who enter versus who exit the funnel as a customer so don't get frustrated when you first start out. And, don't compare your funnel to all of the online experts out there because you will find so many different and varying viewpoints and data on what constitutes a good funnel. What works great in one industry won't in another so you will need to take the basics and tweak until you find what works the best for you. And when you find that perfect funnel, you will be able to ramp it up and your return will be more than you expected. Don't get frustrated but have fun with it because the reward at the end will be worth it.

Module 10 Instagram Advertising

All previous Modules deal with Facebook advertising which was the purpose of the manual. But, did you know that you can advertise on Instagram at the same time you are placing your Facebook ads. In 2012, Facebook purchased Instagram for a whopping $1 Billion. In June of 2018, Instagram the second largest social medial platform and primarily a mobile app, had 1 billion users and it continues to grow. With the integration of Instagram advertising into Facebook, it has become a lot easier to target the mobile market which is where most people spend their time. The cost is typically cheaper than Facebook advertising as well. So, you need to add Instagram advertising to your marketing plan.

You have a choice when creating your ads, keep Facebook and Instagram separate with separate budgets or create them in the same Ad Set and they share the budget. I'm going to outline how to create a basic Instagram ad and will keep them in the same Ad Set with Facebook so that you can see some of the differences you need to plan for, just remember you can do them separately as well.

The first thing we need to do is connect your Instagram account to Facebook by going to the Business Settings and locating Instagram accounts.

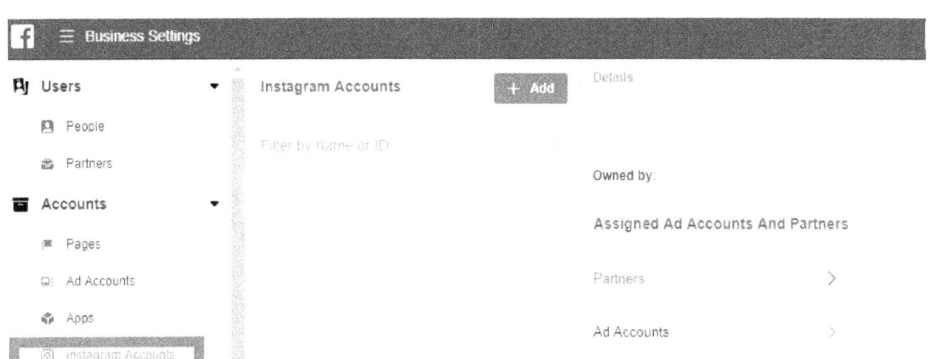

Click on Add and enter your Username and Password for your Instagram account then click Next.

Add an Instagram Account

Enter the username and password for your Instagram account.

Username

Password

Step 1 of 2

Cancel

By clicking Next, you agree to our Terms, Data Policy and Cookies Policy.

Next select the Facebook ad account you want the Instagram to have access to then click Next.

If everything is successful you will get a popup that says Instagram Account Added Successfully.

Instagram Account Added Successfully

Details

Only people who have access to ad accounts assigned to this Instagram account can use it for advertising. New campaigns and ad sets will automatically include Instagram selected as a placement, and you can link new ads to this Instagram account.

Done

You are now ready to create your ad using most of the same steps as Module 2 only this time adapting a few things to accommodate Instagram requirements. If you don't remember how to do a certain task, please review Module 2.

1. Go to Ads Manager and click on Create
2. Pick Traffic for your Marketing Objective and give your Campaign a name.
3. Create your Ad Set Name
4. Pick your Audience
5. Placements is the first spot that you can configure something specific to Instagram. Choose Edit Placements and a list of different platforms will appear that you can place your ad. By default everything is checked which is the same as leaving Automatic Placements checked instead of Edit Placements. You can pick and choose where you want your ad to be displayed. If you are choosing to run

your Instagram with a separate budget from your Facebook ads, then you uncheck all the placements except Instagram.

6. Tell Facebook what your Budget is and how you want to be charged. Remember if you choose to run Facebook and Instagram ads together in the same Ad Set than they will share the same budget.
7. Create your Ad Name
8. Choose Single Image Format
9. Images is the second spot that you can configure to meet Instagram requirements.
    a. Choose your Facebook image which is 1200x628 pixels
    b. Click Use a different image for Instagram under your Facebook image and upload or choose your Instagram image from your library. For images to look correct on Instagram they need to be 1080x1080 pixels.

10. Finish the Link, Text, Headline and other settings as you normally would for a Facebook ad and click Publish.

As you can see, if you know how to create a Facebook ad, then creating an Instagram ad is pretty straight forward. The only differences to remember are that still images need to be 1080x1080 pixels and Instagram videos have a limitation of 15 seconds for Instagram Stories and 60 seconds for Instagram

With Instagram growing at a fast pace, inexpensive advertising, integrated with Facebook advertising and being primarily a mobile platform, which is where most people spend their time, it only makes sense to utilize Instagram advertising. Everything discussed in previous Modules can be adapted to Instagram advertising including the Facebook sales funnel module. Now go and create ads, have fun and have successful marketing plans.

About the Author: Gary has been working in the technology field for over 25 years and is usually the one who is open to finding a way to implement new technology to make business workflows easier and more profitable. Along the way, social media has started to become more integrated with technology and he willingly jumped in order to find how to use the new social media platforms and technology in business to keep up with the rapidly changing times. Having been in leadership roles and a P.P.S. (Professional Problem Solver), Gary has been able to get business to understand that departments such as IT, Marketing and Sales are no longer separate entities but instead must work together for the common goal. He has been successfully running Facebook ads for 4 years with a spent budget to date of over 1 million dollars. Facebook and other platforms are constantly changing which adds to the fun and enjoyment of working in this field because there is always something new to learn and try.

Gary is also the author of:

God's Story: A Foster Child's Story

Modern Leadership: A Companion Guide for Today's Leaders

Both are available on Amazon.

If you want to contact the author, you can do so at gstarr1266@gmail.com.